Y0-EMD-831

SCIENCE OF MIND HYMNAL

Compiled and Edited
by
Thos. L. McClellan

Published by
Tona Music Company
San Marcos, California

SCIENCE OF MIND HYMNAL

November, 1976
First Edition

Printed in the United States of America

PREFACE

This hymnal is yours; read, sing, and joyfully use it. Our purpose has been to provide a complete and meaningful hymnal for Religious Science, and for all other metaphysical groups that seek the refreshing vitality of its text and the inspiring harmony of its music. The text is new, with few exceptions. The music, selected both for formal and informal group singing, comes from many sources and covers a broad spectrum of majestic, meditative, and modern tunes. In response to many requests, effort has been made to provide music with a singable tune and range.

For greater convenience and utility, the 163 songs have been segregated into six basic sections. Also, as a special feature a section containing 29 responsive readings identified under various subject titles has been included at the request of many churches.

To those who have urged us into this project, and to those who have so graciously assisted in its composition, we extend our sincere gratitude. Special appreciation lovingly is given to my wife, Nadene McClellan, for her suggestions and faithful clerical assistance. We also are appreciative to the Rev. Dr. and Mrs. Raymond K. Lilley, the Rev. Helen Seybold, Ernest Tamminga, and Nolan Van Way for their encouragement and helpful detailed review of the hymnal material; to Dr. Norman L. Owen for special assistance as music adviser; and to Musiprint, Mr. and Mrs. Jerrold A. Kiser, and Musicraft for their preparation of the engravings.

We are grateful to the many authors, composers and publishers for their cooperation in granting the use of copyrighted material, and in permitting certain adaptations and abridgements. Specific credits are shown on each selection respectively. We give special recognition to Dr. Willis H. Kinnear and to Science of Mind Magazine for their permission to use certain material included in the responsive reading section; to Harper & Row, Publishers, for the use of a selected portion from "The Gospel According to Thomas" (by Guillaumont, Peuch, Quispel, Till, and Al Masih), copyright by E. J. Brill, 1959.

A diligent search has been made to trace ownership of each work; and if proper credit has been omitted, or incorrectly shown, a correction gladly will be made in future editions of this hymnal upon receipt of written notice.

Thos. L. McClellan
Editor

CONTENTS

SONG SECTIONS (Nos. 1-163)
Acknowledgement and Praise . . . . . 1 – 11
Awareness and Activity . . . . . 12 – 49
Meditation and Prayer . . . . . 50 – 70
Informal and General . . . . . 71 – 133
Special Days and Seasons . . . . . 134 – 150
National and Other . . . . . 151 – 163

DECLARATION OF PRINCIPLES (No. 164)

RESPONSIVE READINGS (Nos. 165-192)
Abundance 165
As Man Thinketh 166
Bondage and Limitation 167
Born Again 168
Charity 169
Choice 170
Christ 171
Communion 172
Faith 173
Gift of God 174
God in All 175
God in Creation 176
God in Man 177
Growth 178
Happiness 179
Healing 180
Immortality 181
Kingdom of God 182
Kinship 183
Love 184
Negation 185
Potential 186
Realization 187
Salvation 188
Trust 189
Truth 190
Unity 191
Works 192

INDEX OF TUNES AND METERS

Adeste Fideles (Irregular) 30
Agni (Irregular) 32
Alford (7.6.7.6.7.6.8.6.) 45
All Saints New (C.M.D.) 4
America (6.6.4.6.6.6.4.) 152
American Melody (C.M.) 77
American Spiritual (Irregular) 130, 132
Amesbury (C.M.D.) 34
Ancient of Days (11.10.11.10) 20
Antioch (C.M.) 148
Ar Hyd Y Nos (8.4.8.4.8.8.8.4.) 35
Assurance (9.10.9.9. with refrain) 73
Austria (8.7.8.7.D) 25, 154
Azmon (C.M.) 79

Battle Hymn (15.15.15.6) 135
Beacon Hill (Irregular) 97
Beatitudo (C.M.) 60
Beecher (8.7.8.7.D) 14, 42
Beloit (L.M.) 9, 43

Chautauqua (7.7.7.7.4. with refrain) 70
Christmas Song (6.6.6.6.12.12.) 150
Coronation (C.M.) 1
CWM Rhondda (8.7.8.7.4.4.7.7.) 41

Diademata (S.M.D.) 2
Dix (7.7.7.7.7.7.) 98
Dolomite Chant (6.6.6.6.) 58

Easter Hymn (7.4.7.4.D) 140
Ellacombe (C.M.D.) 65
Ellers (10.10.10.10.) 69
Evan (C.M.) 31
Eventide (10.10.10.10.) 50

Faben (8.7.8.7.D) 47
Far-Off Lands (7.6.7.6.D) 44
Forest Green (C.M.D.) 39

Gerald (C.M.D.) 61
Gloria (7.7.7.7. with refrain) 147
G.E.M. Govan (Irregular) 24

Hankey (7.6.7.6.D with refrain) 80
He Leadeth (8.8.8.8. with refrain) 83

Hursley (L.M.) 142
Hymn to Joy (8.7.8.7.D) 21, 28

In Babilone (8.7.8.7.D) 67
Italian Hymn – See Trinity 15

Kingsfold (C.M.D.) 26, 38
Kremser (12.11.13.12.) 144

Lacquiparle (Irregular) 112
Lancashire (7.6.7.6.D) 23, 138
Latin Spring Hymn (7.6.7.6.D) 139
Leave Me With a Smile (Irregular) 160
Lyons (10.10.11.11.) 6, 46

Maori Melody (10.10.10.10.) 84
Materna (C.M.D.) 19, 151
Melita (8.8.8.8.8.8.) 5, 27
Mendebras (7.6.7.6.D) 49
Mendelssohn (7.7.7.7.D with refrain) 145

Mercy (7.7.7.7.) 52
Morecambe (10.10.10.10.) 63
Munich (7.6.7.6.D) 36

National Hymn (10.10.10.10.) 18
Nettleton (8.7.8.7.D) 123

Nicaea (Irregular) 7, 16
Nun Danket (6.7.6.7.6.6.6.6.) 141

O Mi Querida (Irregular) 96
Old Hundredth (L.M.) 162

Picardy (Irregular) 156
Prayer (11.10.11.10) 62
Pues Adios Hasta Ki (Irregular) 94

Regent Square (8.7.8.7.8.7.) 13
Rest (8.6.8.8.6.) 33
Russian Hymn (11.10.11.9.) 3

St. Asaph (8.7.8.7.D) 22, 40
St. Catherine (8.8.8.8.8.8.) 155
St. George's Windsor (7.7.7.7.D) 143
St. Gertrude (6.5.6.5.D) 76
St. Leonard (Hiles) (C.M.D.) 37
St. Louis (8.6.8.6.7.6.8.6.) 149
Serenity (C.M.) 81
Slane (10.10.9.10.) 17
Spanish Hymn (7.7.7.7.D) 10
Stille Nacht (Irregular) 146
Swedish Folk Melody (Irregular) 8
Sweet Hour (L.M.D.) 57
Swing Low (Irregular) 131

Tempus Adest Floridum (7.6.7.6.D) 139
Terra Beata (S.M.D.) 11
Trentham (S.M.) 51
Trinity (6.6.4.6.6.6.4.) 15

Viennese Melody (10.10.10.10.) 120

Waltham (L.M.) 136
Webb (7.6.7.6.D) 48, 137
Weimar (8.4.8.4.8.8.8.4.) 12
Welwyn (11.10.11.10.) 64

GENERAL INDEX

(Titles are in CAPS; first lines in lower case type)

A GOLDEN DAWN IS BREAKING 23
A THOUSAND WAYS 34
ABIDE WITH ME 50
ALL HAIL THE POWER 1
AMERICA THE BEAUTIFUL 151
ANCIENT OF DAYS 20
ANGELS WE HAVE HEARD ON HIGH 147
ARE YOU READY, WILLING AND ABLE 106
As I behold Thy mighty works 8
Awake! awake! and sing 71
AWAKENING CHORUS 71

BE THOU MY VISION 17
BELIEVE AND KNOW 114
BREATHE ON ME, BREATH OF GOD 51

CHRIST, THE LORD IS RISEN TODAY 140
COME, YE THANKFUL PEOPLE, COME 143
CREATIVE AND SUSTAINING SOURCE 5
CREATOR OF THE UNIVERSE 4

DAY IS DYING IN THE WEST 70
DEAR LORD AND FATHER OF MANKIND 33
DECLARATION THEME SONG 163
Deep as the ocean 89
Do you know what 161
DOWN DEEP IN YOUR HEART 129
DOXOLOGY 162

EACH DAY I'LL LIVE ANEW 99
ETERNAL MIND 61
EVER SO WONDROUSLY 59

FAITH OF OUR FATHERS 155
FATHER, TO US THY CONSTANT LOVE 62
FOR THE BEAUTY OF THE EARTH 98
FORWARD I WALK WITH GOD 24
FREEDOM 68
FROM GLORY UNTO GLORY 45
From now on I'll walk 111
FROM THIS MOMENT ON 134

GIVE A LITTLE MORE 122
GLORIOUS IS THE TEMPLE STANDING 25
Go not, my soul, in search of Him 26
God has a thousand ways to bring 34
God is all Power 78
GOD IS GROWING IN ME 94
GOD IS MY PERFECT LIFE 120
GOD IS OUR REFUGE 66
God is the Life 127
GOD IS THE SOURCE 73
GOD OF LOVE FORE'ER INDWELLING 14
GOD OF OUR FATHERS 18
GOD REALLY LIVES 82
GOD THE OMNIPOTENT 3
GOD'S CONSTANCY 83
GOD'S LOVE IS DEEP WITHIN ME 131
GOD'S LOVING LIGHT 86
GOD'S MELODY OF LIFE 126
GREAT SHEPHERD OF ALL 79
GUIDE ME, O THOU LIVING PRESENCE 41

HARK! THE HERALD ANGELS SING 145
HAVE A HAPPY HEART 125
HAVE YOU EVER SEEN THE BEAUTY 97
HE THAT EVERY SUN UPHOLDETH 13
HE THAT GOETH FORTH WITH VISION 67
HEAR THE CHURCH BELLS RINGING 74
HOLY, HOLY, HOLY 7
HOLY SPIRIT, TRUTH DIVINE 52
How marvelous, how wonderful 105

I AM 111
I am God's melody of life 126
I AM THE SHEPHERD 39
I CAN SING ABOUT THE GLORIES 121
I come to the garden alone 87
I HAVE A SHIP 38
I have the joy, joy, joy, joy 93
I have the light of Life 128
I HEAR THY VOICE 53
I LOVE TO TELL THE STORY 80
I PRAISE THE WEALTH OF GOD 72
I RADIATE THE LOVE 91
I REMEMBER 85
I WOULD EVER WALK WITH THEE 130
If I falter in life's throng 130
If you really love and sing 129
IMMORTAL LOVE 65
IN-A MY HEART 132
IN EACH PATHWAY WE ARE WENDING 12
IN MY HEART THERE'S A SONG 119
IN THE GARDEN 87
IN THE TWINKLING OF AN EYE 107
IN TRUTH BE THY TRUST 46
INDWELLING GOD 84
INTERNATIONAL HYMN 21
IT IS LOVE 161
IT IS TRUE 108
IT SOUNDS ALONG THE AGES 75
I'VE WANDERED 101

JESUS, MAY ALL MEN AWAKEN 47
JOY IN MY HEART 93
JOY TO THE WORLD 148
JOYFUL, JOYFUL, WE ADORE THEE 28

KNOWING 102
KUM BA YAH 159

LET ALL WHO ENTER 156
LET GO, LET GOD 115
LET THERE BE PEACE ON EARTH 158
LET'S BE 113
LIFE IS FOR LIVING 117
LIFE WITHIN IS SPIRIT 16
Lord, I want to be more loving 132
LORD OF THE UNIVERSE 2
LOVE 90
LOVE DIVINE, ALL LOVE EXCELLING 42

MAY OUR HEARTS BE ALWAYS OPEN 133
Mine eyes have seen the coming 135
MY COUNTRY 'TIS OF THEE 152
MY CREATIVE INTENTION 110
MYSTERIOUS PRESENCE, SOURCE OF ALL 74

NEW AGE VISION 135
NO SEPARATION 77
NOT SO IN HASTE, MY HEART! 58
NOW POWER 116
NOW THANK WE ALL OUR GOD 141

O beautiful for spacious skies 151
O BROTHER MAN, FOLD TO THY HEART 64
O CHRIST, THOU GREAT EXAMPLE 37
O DAY OF LIGHT AND GLADNESS 138
O FAITH THAT LIGHTS THE SOUL 27
O HOLY FATHER, GOD OF ALL 19
O LITTLE TOWN OF BETHLEHEM 149
O LOVE OF GOD 43
O MIGHTY GOD, THY SPIRIT ONE 60
O PRAISE YE THE ONE 6
O say, can you see 153
O there is Now Power 116
O THOU ALMIGHTY GOD 15
O THOU GREAT AND MIGHTY FATHER 40
O THOU, IN ALL THY MIGHT SO FAR 81
O Thou who art the God of all 9
O THOU, WHOSE POWER 69
ONWARD SOULS ETERNAL 76
OPEN MY EYES THAT I MAY SEE 55
OURS, O LORD, A MIGHTY NATION 154
OVER THE MOUNTAIN 127

Praise God that Good is everywhere 162

RING OUT THE OLD, RING IN THE NEW 136
RISE UP, YE PEOPLE 29

Seek and find 163
SING A SONG 124
Sing and have a happy heart 125
SING! O SING, YE JOYFUL PEOPLE 22
SPIRIT OF GOD 56
SPIRIT OF GOD, AWAKEN NOW MY HEART 63
Spirit of Life eternal 56
SPRING HAS NOW UNWRAPPED 139
STAY ALIVE 118
SWEET HOUR OF PRAYER 57

TEMPER MY SPIRIT, O LORD 32
THE INDWELLING SPIRIT 26
THE HEAVENS DECLARE THY GLORY 44
THE HOPE OF NATIONS 137
THE LORD IS IN HIS HOLY TEMPLE 157
THE LORD'S MY SHEPHERD 31
THE LOVE OF GOD IN MAN 89
THE MORN OF TRUTH IS BREAKING 49
THE STAR-SPANGLED BANNER 153
THE TRUTH MAKES US FREE 30
There is a nature within every one 108
THERE SHALL BE SHOWERS OF BLESSING 103
There's a Creative Intention 110
THERE'S A SONG IN THE AIR 150
THEY'LL KNOW AND BELIEVE IT 92
THIS I BELIEVE 78
THIS IS MY FATHER'S WORLD 11
THIS IS YOU 105
THOU, CHRIST OF GOD, INDWELLING 36
Thou whose breathing fills 21
THOU WHOSE SPIRIT DWELLS IN ALL 10
THOU WILT KEEP HIM IN PERFECT PEACE 54
THROUGH THE LOVE OF GOD 35
THY PRAISE I SING 8

WALKING IN SPIRIT 96
We are one in the Spirit 92
WE BUILD A NEW TOMORROW 48
WE COME WITH REJOICING 144
WE GO NOW IN PEACE 160
WE PRAISE THEE FATHER 9
WE PRAISE THEE, O GOD 104
We sing the hope of nations 137
WE THANK THEE, LORD, FOR THIS 142
What a glorious thought 102
WHAT GREATER PEARL 112
WHEN I REMEMBER 100
When my world seems cold 100
When Truth in its beauty 30
WHEN TWILIGHT SHADOWS END THE DAY 88
WHISPER A PRAYER 95
WHY 123
With many a trial 94
With the service ending 160
WITHIN MY HEART 128

YOU CAN SMILE 109
You have seen the forests 68

All Hail the Power

CORONATION

Henry Victor Morgan

Oliver Holden, 1793

1. All hail the Pow'r of Truth to save From er - ror's bind-ing thrall. Let joy - ful songs of praise a - bound, For God is All in All. Let joy - ful songs of praise a - bound, For God is All in All.
2. Let all whose hearts are heav - en turned List to the Spir - it's call. Know that our God is e'er the same, And Love is Lord of all. Know that our God is e'er the same, And Love is Lord of all.
3. One God and Fa - ther of us all, There is no great nor small. In Him we live and move and breathe, And Love is Lord of all. In Him we live and move and breathe, And Love is Lord of all.

From "Religious Science Hymnal". Used by permission of Dodd, Mead & Co.

2 Lord of the Universe

Christina Hovemann

DIADEMATA
George J. Elvey

1. Lord of the u - ni - verse, Of all things, great and small,
2. Lord of the u - ni - verse, Yet one with ev - ery cell,
3. Lord of the u - ni - verse, The sub-stance of all things,

Su - preme in heav - en and on earth, In - deed the Lord of all!
Thy love and great in - tel - li - gence With - in all things doth dwell:
Thou art the spir - it and the life That makes our soul take wings!

We mag - ni - fy Thy name, As won-ders we be - hold,
Thou art in ev - ery star, In ev - ery stick and stone,
Let now our thoughts as - cend To that ce - les - tial height

And cher-ish in our hu - man hearts Thy glo - ries man - i - fold.
And clos - er still, with - in each heart Thou art the Lord a - lone.
Where love and peace and joy a - bound, A - long with truth and light.

God the Omnipotent 3

Based on Henry F. Chorley
John Ellerton, and others
RUSSIAN HYMN
Alexis F. Lvov
1. God the Om - nip - o - tent, Spir - it or - dain - ing
Cre - a - tion's glo - ry, so might - y thy word;
Through - out all space is thy law ev - er reign - ing
Praise be to Thee for all time, O Lord.
2. God Om - ni - pres - ent, man has for - sak - en
Thy ways of bless - ed - ness, slight - ed thy word;
Bid that the hearts of all men now a - wak - en
To know thy peace for all time, O Lord.
3. God the Om - nis - cient, thy light re - leas - ing,
Earth shall to free - dom and truth be re - stored;
Dis - pell - ing dark - ness, thy king - dom un - ceas - ing
Shall bring true peace for all time, O Lord. A - men.

4 Creator of the Universe

ALL SAINTS NEW
J. Donald Hughes
Henry S. Cutler
1. Cre-a - tor of the un - i - verse, We lift our minds to thee;
2. Let not the love of eas - y ways Leave deep-er truth un - known;
En-light-en them and lead our thought In fear-less lib - er - ty.
Teach us that pow'r to learn and grow Is found in thee a - lone.
Let not our search for truth in things From thee our souls di - vide;
Let sci - ence find in thee its truth; Tech-nol - o - gy, its Goal;
Thou art the liv - ing Lord of truth; Thy Spir - it be our guide!
Phi - los - o - phy, its no - blest tho't: Thy light makes know-ledge whole!

Creative and Sustaining Source 5

MELITA

Thos L. McClellan — John B. Dykes

1. Cre - a - tive and Sus - tain - ing Source, Thru thee all life shall
2. With break of dawn a - ware - ness shows The wis-dom that all
3. Great God, thy pow - er e'er shall be The glo - ry of e-
find its course; As warmth of thy e - ter - nal ray
na - ture knows; The seed that feeds on thine own gifts,
ter - ni - ty; Each at - om of all time and space
Ex - pands to wel - come each new day, The glo - ry of all
In glo - ry and in beau - ty lifts; And as thy light is
Is thy cre - a - tion filled with grace; And en - er-gized to
life un- folds, Re - vealed with - in re - fresh - ened molds.
seen by men, A - wak - ened spir - its live a - gain.
reach its goal, Di - vine - ly acts, re - veals the soul. A - men.

6 O Praise Ye the One

Robert Grant, adapted

LYONS
From William Gardiner's
Sacred Melodies, 1815

1. O praise ye the One, Who won-drous-ly reigns, Let
2. O sing of his might, And sing of his grace, Whose
3. O praise ye the store Of won-ders un - told, The
prais-es be sung, In joy - ful re - frains, To
robe is the light, Whose can - o-py space; Cre-
man-i-fold gifts God's love doth un - fold; His
God our de - fend - er, Our source and de - sign, So
a - tion re - veal - eth His spir - it in form, And
Spir - it in - dwells us, For - ev - er to bless, How
ra - diant in splen - dor And wis - dom di - vine.
of his own es - sence Each new day is born.
end - less the mea - sure Of His giv - ing - ness.

Holy, Holy, Holy

Composite from
Reginald Heber, 1826,
and others

NICAEA
John B. Dykes, 1861

1. Ho - ly, ho - ly, ho - ly, Lord God Al - might - y!
2. Ho - ly, ho - ly, ho - ly, dark- ness can - not hide Thee,
3. Ho - ly, ho - ly, ho - ly, all our hearts a - dore Thee,

Ear - ly in the morn - ing our song shall rise to Thee;
All thy works shall praise thy name in earth and sky and sea;
Liv - ing in Love's full - ness through - out e - ter - ni - ty;

Ho - ly, ho - ly, ho - ly, mer - ci-ful and might - y;
Thou a - lone art ho - ly, there is none be - side Thee,
What can sep - a - rate Thee From the heart that seeks Thee!

Who was, and is, and ev - er - more shall be.
Per - fect in pow'r, in love and u - ni - ty.
This through all a - ges ev - er - more shall be.

Thy Praise I Sing

Based on Psalm 104
Thos. L. McClellan

Swedish Folk Melody
Arr. by Thos. L. McClellan

1. As I be - hold Thy might - y works en - thrall - ing, And see the
2. I see the sun a - glow on tow'r - ing moun - tains, And soon the
3. And when I think that God in man de - sir - ing, Re - veals to
pow'r of Thy cre - a - tive law; In sea - sons green, or when the leaves are
night is ra - di - ant with stars Re - flect - ed in the lakes, and streams like
him the way from stress and strife; O joy - ous thought, my con - scious - ness ac -
fall - ing, My wak - ened soul re - sponds in rev - erent awe.
foun - tains; How man - i - fold Thy great cre - a - tions are.
quir - ing: God's gift to man is more a - bun - dant life.
Refrain
Thy praise I sing, O Lord, my God to Thee, Thou art all

pow - er; all har-mo - ny; Thy praise I sing with-in my soul to
Thee, Thou art my life, my des - ti - ny.

We Praise Thee, Father 9

BELOIT

Thos. L. McClellan — Carl G. Reissiger

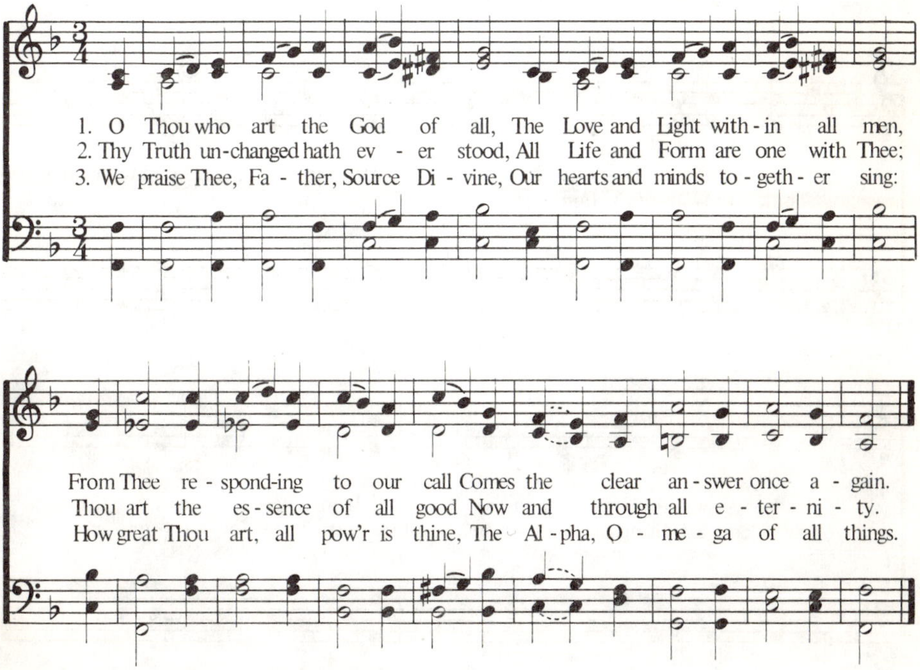

1. O Thou who art the God of all, The Love and Light with - in all men,
2. Thy Truth un-changed hath ev - er stood, All Life and Form are one with Thee;
3. We praise Thee, Fa - ther, Source Di - vine, Our hearts and minds to - geth - er sing:

From Thee re - spond-ing to our call Comes the clear an - swer once a - gain.
Thou art the es - sence of all good Now and through all e - ter - ni - ty.
How great Thou art, all pow'r is thine, The Al - pha, O - me - ga of all things.

10 Thou Whose Spirit Dwells in All

John W. Chadwick, 1890
Alt. and abridged

SPANISH HYMN
Arranged by Benjamin Carr, 1824

1. Thou whose spir-it dwells in all, Pri - mal source of life and mind,
2. Proph - et - soul in ev - ery kind, Hid - den force of all we see;
In the earth as in the soul, Ev - er full and un - con - fined!
Vig - or and e - ter - nal quest Of life's true po - lar - i - ty.
What shall sep - a - rate from Thee? Noth - ing of cre - a - ted things!
Thine the at-om's faint-est pulse, Thine the cy - cles as be - fore;
Beau - ty, wis-dom, pow'r and joy, Each from Thee its es-sence brings.
Se - cret of things yet to be, Life with Thee for - ev - er - more.

This Is My Father's World

TERRA BEATA
Traditional English Melody
Arr. Franklin L. Sheppard

Maltbie D. Babcock, alt.

1. This is my Fa-ther's world; And to my lis-tening ears, All
2. This is my Fa-ther's world; The birds their car - ols raise, The
3. This is my Fa-ther's world; Oh, let me ne'er for - get That
na - ture sings, and 'round me rings The mu - sic of the spheres. This
morn - ing light, the lil - y white De - clare their Mak-er's praise. This
though the wrong seems oft so strong, God is the Rul-er yet. This
is my Fa-ther's world; I rest me in the thought Of
is my Fa-ther's world; He shines in all that's fair; In the
is my Fa-ther's world; Why should my heart be low? His
rocks and trees, of skies and seas, His hand the won-ders wrought.
rus-tling grass I hear him pass, He speaks to me ev-ery-where.
na - ture fair, each one may share, And all His glo-ry know.

12 In Each Pathway We Are Wending

WEIMAR

William E. Hickson, adapted

Arr. from a German Chorale

1. In each path-way we are wend-ing, God speed the right!
2. Now in con-scious-ness ap-pear-ing, God speed the right!
3. Still our on-ward course pur-su-ing, God speed the right!
To each thought we are at-tend-ing, God speed the right!
No con-di-tion ev-er fear-ing, God speed the right!
Ev-ery foe at length sub-du-ing, God speed the right!
May we live our lives be-fore Thee, Find the truth as those in sto-ry,
Pains and tri-als are re-ced-ing, And no long-er are im-ped-ing,
Truth, thy cause, what-e'er de-lay it, There's no pow'r on earth can stay it,
Know the full-ness of thy glo-ry, God speed the right!
As the truth we now are heed-ing, God speed the right!
Proud-ly now we shall o-bey it, God speed the right! A-men.

He That Every Sun Upholdeth

REGENT SQUARE

Thomas H. Gill, adapted

Henry T. Smart

1. He that ev - ery sun up-hold - eth, Gives to man his
2. Nev - er is his pow - er flaunt - ed, His the ways for -
3. On - ward, up - ward doth He beck - on, On - ward, up - ward
guid - ing hand; He that a - ges hath un-fold - eth,
ev - er sure; And with heart and mind un-daunt - ed,
would we press; In his wis - dom we would reck - on,
Shall our ways in truth ex - pand; God or - dain - ing,
We ex - press his es - sence pure; God all know-ing,
In his truth our strength pos - sess; God is giv - ing,
e'er sus - tain-ing, In his strength and stay we stand.
e'er be - stow-ing, Ends our er - ror and its lure.
in us liv - ing, And his love shall ev - er bless. A - men.

14 God of Love Fore'er Indwelling

Thos. L. McClellan

BEECHER
John Zundel, 1870

1. God of Love for - e'er in - dwell-ing, Joy to ev - ery
2. God of Love so ev - er near us, More re - cep - tive
3. God of Love, E - ter - nal Spir - it, Give to men Thy
trou - bled heart! In Thy bound - less lov - ing spir - it
we would be, Know - ing in our true ful - fill - ment
strong in - tent, When they seek Thy high - er mer - it
Each new mo - ment takes it's part To re - move de -
That all bless - ings come from Thee; Com - ing with e -
All their deeds are heav - en sent. Peace be to this
struc - tive forc - es By which men lose self - con - trol;
man - ci - pa - tion By the truth we long have sought;
con - gre - ga - tion, And in ev - ery heart be known;
While the con-stance
Com-ing with the
And with faith and

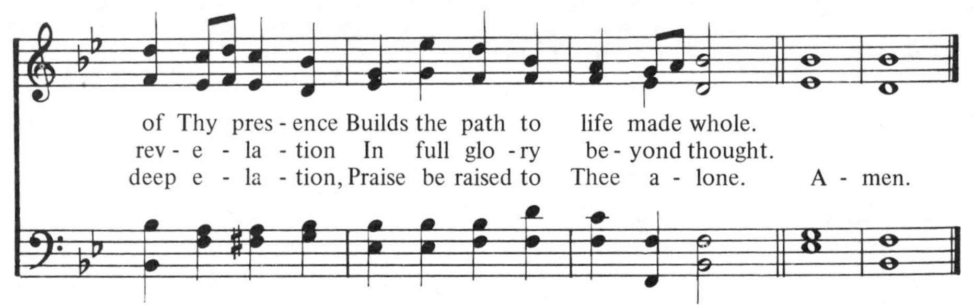
of Thy pres - ence Builds the path to life made whole.
rev - e - la - tion In full glo - ry be - yond thought.
deep e - la - tion, Praise be raised to Thee a - lone. A - men.

O Thou Almighty God

15

TRINITY

Anonymous before 1757, adapted

Felice Giardini, 1769, adapted

1. O Thou Al - might - y God, Light-ing the path we trod,
2. O Thou In - car - nate One, Let all thy truth be done,
3. Rule Thou in ev - ery soul, And in each heart be whole,

We sing thy praise; Fa - ther, all - glo - ri - ous, O'er all vic -
Our thoughts in - spire; And all thy peo - ple bless, Giv - ing thy
Hence ev - er - more; Rul - ing in ma - jes - ty, May we thy

to - ri - ous, Thy love re - stor - eth us From bar - ren ways.
word suc-cess, Spir - it of be - ing-ness Our liv - ing fire.
glo - ry see, And to e - ter - ni-ty Love and a - dore.

16 Life Within Is Spirit

Clarence Mayer

NICAEA
John B. Dykes, 1861

1. Life with - in is Spir - it, nev - er fail - ing foun - tain,
2. Life with - in a - bid - ing; this is Life E - ter - nal;
3. Life with - in is Pow - er, I am nev - er daunt - ed;
Ris - ing up with - in my soul, meets each e - mer - gen - cy.
Through the stress and storm of life, my peace re - sides with - in.
For I know God's Love and Law reign through me ev - er - more.
From with - in re - mov - ing, e'en though like a moun - tain,
I go forth cou - ra - geous; Joy is mine sup - er - nal;
Life with - in is Spir - it; Truth can - not be flaunt - ed;
All un - like Spir - it all in har - mo - ny.
Fear - less, I con - quer; I go forth to win.
Heav - en and earth are one for - ev - er - more.

Be Thou My Vision 17

Ancient Irish
Trans. by Mary E. Byrne
Versified by Eleanor H. Hull

SLANE
Patrick W. Joyce
Harm. by David Evans

1. Be Thou my Vi - sion, O Lord of my heart;
2. Be Thou my Wis - dom, and Thou my true Word;
3. Rich - es I heed not, nor man's emp - ty praise,
4. High King of heav - en, my vic - to - ry won,
Naught be all else to me, save that Thou art—
I ev - er with Thee and Thou with me, Lord;
Thou mine in - her - it - ance, now and al - ways;
May I reach heav - en's joys, O bright heaven's Sun!
Thou my best thought, by day or by night,
Thou my great Fa - ther, I Thy true son;
Thou and Thou on - ly, first in my heart,
Heart of my own heart, what - ev - er be - fall,
Wak - ing or sleep - ing, Thy pres - ence my light.
Thou in me dwell - ing, and I with Thee one.
High King of heav - en, my Treas - ure Thou art.
Still be my Vi - sion, O Rul - er of all. A - men.

18 God of Our Fathers, Whose Almighty Hand

Daniel C. Roberts, 1876, adapted

NATIONAL HYMN
George W. Warren, 1894

Trumpets, before each stanza
(Optional)
1. God of our fa - thers, whose al - might - y hand, Leads forth in beau - ty all the star-ry band Of shin - ing worlds in splen - dor through the skies, Our song of praise in grat - i - tude a - rise.
2. Thy pow'r and grace has led us in the past, And in our life, Thy love and law are cast; Thou art our vi - sion, and in - tel - li - gence, Our mind in Thine our ev - er sure de - fense.
3. Thy love re - fresh - es from our toil - some way, Thy law re - moves the night with glo-rious day, Thy life gives strength in ev - ery cir - cum - stance, In faith we live with - out a back - ward glance. A - men.

O Holy Father, God of All 19

MATERNA
Samuel Augustus Ward, 1882
Arranged

Thos. L. McClellan

1. O Ho - ly Fa - ther, God of all, In - cline our tho'ts to Thee,
2. With - in the qui - et of our soul, With all e - mo - tions still,
3. O God Di - vine, how great Thou art Be - yond the tho'ts of man,
And fill our hearts and minds this day With love's true har - mo - ny;
A - wak - en our a - ware - ness to Thy per - fect law and will;
In - dwell - ing all, im - pell - ing all, Be - fore the world be - gan;
'Til Thy di - vine ac - tiv - i - ty With wis - dom clear shall rise,
Sus - tained with full as - sur - ance, Lord, Let faith for - ev - er bless,
May all be - lieve with Christ - like mind, 'Til time shall be no more,
Dis - pell - ing way - ward at - ti - tudes That dim our search - ing eyes.
As Spir - it finds re - birth a - gain With - in our con - scious - ness.
Thy king - dom lives with - in all men To know and to a - dore.

Ancient of Days

ANCIENT OF DAYS
William C. Doane, 1886; adapted
J. Albert Jeffery, 1886
1. An - cient of Days that gives to life its glo - ry,
2. O Ho - ly Spir - it, know - ing - ness en - hanc - ing,
3. O Lord of Life, the u - ni - verse de - clar - ing,
We see thy works dis - played in full ar - ray;
To Thee we owe the all in - spir - ing pow'r;
Thou art the es - sence giv - ing full re - lease;
Thou e'er has blessed cre - a - tion's won - drous sto - ry
Beam - ing thy Light to guide each soul ad - vanc - ing,
In us there flows thy Pow - er now pre - par - ing,
With love and light, since the first dawn - ing day.
And bring - ing calm with - in the dark - est hour.
The thought and word that guides our way to peace. A - men.

Word adaptation © 1972, 1976 Thos. L. McClellan. Used by permission.

International Hymn

Angela Morgan

HYMN TO JOY
Ludwig van Beethoven, 1823, adapted

1. Thou whose breath-ing fills our bod - ies, Thou whose pulse the worlds o - bey,
2. Thou whose or - der rules the a - tom, Thou whose law pro - pels the sea,
3. Thou who light - est with Thy glo - ry Leaf and lake and cloud and star,

Tune our minds to heed Thy rhy - thm Known a - long the star - ry way.
Bring, oh, bring Thy war - ring peo - ples Close with-in Thy har - mo - ny.
Light the hearts of men to jus - tice, Show us kin - dred, as we are.

Swing the na - tions to Thy meas-ure, Bid men's ha-tred turn to song;
God of beau - ty, heal our mad-ness! God of love, our bat - tles end!
Pour Thy might - y joy up - on us, Thou whose gran-deur fill - eth space,

Fill us, thrill us, with Thy mu - sic, End earth's bit-ter - ness and wrong.
Show the un - i - ty that binds us, Foe to foe, or friend to friend.
Claim Thy cos - mic Sons and Daugh-ters, Un - i - fy the hu - man race!

22 Sing! O Sing, Ye Joyful People

Christina Hovemann, adapted

ST. ASAPH
William S. Bambridge

1. Sing! O sing ye joy - ful peo-ple, Lift-ing high your joy - ful song;
2. Wake, O wake and see per- fec-tion Man- i - fest in ev - ery part;
3. Praise ye the e - ter - nal Spir - it, Might-y and ful - fill - ing pow'r;

Ring the bells from ev - 'ry stee-ple, Sing your prais - es full and strong.
Out - ward - ly in all cre - a - tion, In - ward - ly in ev - ery heart.
Wise men ev - er shall re - vere it In each new ad - vanc-ing hour.

In the tones of mu - sic blend - ing, Hear God's vi - brant har-mo-ny;
With tri - um - phant joy e - ter - nal, Seek and know and ev - er find;
In the light of Truth ex - pand - ing, Great - er vi - sion now be-hold;

And the rhythm It is send-ing Of new glo-ries yet to be.
Jus - ti - fied not by ex - ter - nal, But by at - ti - tude of mind.
And in full - er un-der-stand-ing, Know God's glo-ries man-i- fold. A - men.

A Golden Dawn Is Breaking

LANCASHIRE

Christina Hovemann — Henry T. Smart, 1836

1. A gold - en dawn is break - ing, The shades of night will flee,
2. The gold - en day is dawn - ing, And light of truth ap - pears,
3. The gold - en day ad - vanc - ing, Now sheds a won - drous light,

And sons of men a - wak - ing, The light of truth shall see.
The first bright ray of morn - ing Dis - pels our dark - est fears;
And rays of truth en - hanc - ing Make all things pure and bright;

We hail its light with glad - ness, Our hearts burst in - to song,
With peace and lov - ing kind - ness Trans-form - ing ev - ery heart,
The sons of men, be - hold - ing, Find great - er goals to win,

For truth will con - quer sad - ness, And joy shall reign ere long.
The day of joy and glad - ness Shall nev - er more de - part.
For now we see un fold - ing The light of God with - in!

24 Forward I Walk with God

G. E. M. GOVAN
Ilomay B. Sims — Faith Mission, Edinburgh

1. For-ward I walk with God. For-ward I walk with God. I tra-vel
2. His ways to me are shown, His pow'r is now my own. His Pres-ence

on-ward, My eyes look up-ward For I walk with God.
in me is Health and Glo-ry For I walk with God.

His Truth is my pro - tec-tion. His word is my di - rec-tion, His love up-
So I go sing-ing on-ward, Yes I go sing-ing on-ward I'm reach-ing

holds me. His peace en- folds me For I walk with God.
up-ward, I'm march-ing for-ward For I walk with God.

Words adapted from "Unafraid" by G. E. M. Govan. Used by permission.

Glorious Is the Temple Standing 25

John Newton, adapted

AUSTRIA
Franz Joseph Haydn, 1797

1. Glo - rious is the tem-ple stand-ing, Where man is he stands with God;
2. There the streams of liv -ing wa - ters, Spring-ing from e - ter - nal love,
3. In this tem - ple so per-fect - ed, May our hearts more search-ing be;
One in spir - it e'er ex - pand - ing, Where - so - ev - er man may trod;
Will sup-ply thee, sons and daugh-ters, And all fear and want re-move;
Let our thoughts be more re - flect - ed Toward the truth we seek to see;
With God in thy tem - ple found-ed, What can shake thy sure re-pose;
Who can faint while such a ri - ver, Ev - er will thy thirst as-suage;
Glo - rious things shall then be spo - ken, In our be - ing and our mode;
Though with-out thou be sur-round-ed, God with-in o'er-comes all foes.
Grace which like the Lord, the gi - ver, Nev - er fails from age to age.
And the word shall not be bro - ken, Formed with-in God's own a - bode.

26 The Indwelling Spirit

KINGSFOLD
Vs. 1 & 2 - Frederick L. Hosmer
Vs. 3 - Thos. L. McClellan
Melody coll. Lucy Broadwood
Arr. & harm. R. Vaughan Williams
1. Go not, my soul, in search of Him, Thou wilt not find Him there
2. Thought an-swer-eth a - lone to thought, And soul with soul hath kin;
3. Seek not thy God near yon - der star, Nor search be - yond the sun;
Or in the depths of shad-ows dim, Or heights of up - per air.
The out-ward God he find - eth not, Who finds not God with - in.
The God of love is where you are, Thou art the im - aged one.
For not in far - off realms of space The Spir-it hath its throne;
And if the vi - sion comes to thee, Re - vealed by in-ward sign,
So wan-der not in search of Him, But to thy-self re - pose,
In ev - ery heart it find-eth place, And wait-eth to be known.
Earth will be full of De - i - ty, And with his glo - ry shine.
Where si - lent rev-'rence reigns with-in, And thy a-ware-ness knows. A-men.

O Faith That Lights the Soul of Man 27

Thos. L. McClellan

MELITA
John B. Dykes

1. O faith that lights the soul of man, Im - part - ing hope through-
2. O liv - ing faith in us re - veal The ev - i - dence of
3. O faith di - vine, cre - ate, re - new, Bring new per-spec - tives
out life's span, As - cend now like re - kin - dled fire,
great - er zeal, Im - plant the quest with - in each mind
in - to view, So men may live, be - lieve, and move,
Re - lease all doubt, be - lief in-spire; Be - come that sub-stance,
To lift and glo - ri - fy man-kind; To know the depth of
Ac - cept - ing where they can - not prove; And be that ram - part
though not seen, That glows with - in the heart se - rene.
God's own plan That brings a - bun - dant life to man.
of each soul, The Christ - like faith that mak - est whole. A - men.

28 Joyful, Joyful, We Adore Thee

HYMN TO JOY
Henry Van Dyke, 1908
Ludwig van Beethoven, 1823; adapted
1. Joy - ful, joy - ful, we a - dore thee, God of glo - ry, Lord of love;
2. All thy works with joy sur-round thee, Earth and heaven re - flect thy rays,
3. Thou art giv - ing and for - giv - ing, Ev - er bless-ing, ev - er blest,
4. Mor - tals, join the might - y cho-rus, Which the morn-ing stars be-gan;
Hearts un - fold like flowers be - fore thee, Hail thee as the sun a - bove.
Stars and an - gels sing a - round thee, Cen - ter of un - bro - ken praise;
Well-spring of the joy of liv - ing, O - cean depth of hap - py rest.
Fa - ther love is reign - ing o'er us, Broth - er love binds man to man.
Melt the clouds of sin and sad - ness; Drive the dark of doubt a - way;
Field and for - est, vale and moun-tain, Blos-soming mead-ow, flash-ing sea,
Thou our Fa - ther, Christ our broth - er, All who live in love are thine;
Ev - er sing - ing march we on-ward, Vic-tors in the midst of strife;
Giv - er of im - mor - tal glad-ness, Fill us with the light of day.
Chant-ing bird, and flow - ing foun-tain Call us to re - joice in thee.
Teach us how to love each oth - er, Lift us to the joy di-vine.
Joy - ful mu - sic lifts us sun-ward In the tri - umph song of life.

Rise Up, Ye People

Fenwicke L. Holmes

Toni Roelofsma

1. Rise up, rise up, ye peo - ple, And sing a joy - ful song,
2. Rise up, rise up, ye peo - ple, Let all the call o - bey;
Lift high your voice in glad - ness, Your hap - py notes pro - long.
The blind, the deaf, the fee - ble Shall stand in strength to - day.
For God be - stows His plen - ty In meas - ure un - re - strained;
The Christ with - in is speak - ing; "The Truth shall set you free;
His wealth is for His chil - dren, His boun - ty un - con - tained.
Who feels my pres - ence in him, Shall walk by faith in Me."

30 The Truth Makes Us Free

Ida May Skinner

ADESTE FIDELES
John F. Wade?, 1740

1. When Truth in its beau - ty, Re - splen - dent and clear,
2. When deep - ly with - in us A still voice is heard,
3. Be still then and know That the glo - ry su - per - nal
Re - veals its per - fec - tion, Dis - solv - ing our fear,
And In - fin - ite Spir - it Re - sponds to our word,
Il - lu - mines our path - way, Our spir - its en - thrall,
Then free from all bond - age Our souls then shall be,
And brings to per - fec - tion Our vi - sions to be,
Our lives are re - deemed, And the Truth we shall see,
Our liv - ing ex - press - ing, Our spir - its pos - sess - ing
All er - ror dis - pell - ing, Our firm faith im - pell - ing,
Our faith ev - er grow - ing, Our lives ev - er show - ing

From "Religious Science Hymnal". Used by permission of Dodd, Mead & Co.

The joy of the bless - ing That Truth makes us free.
The Fa - ther in - dwell - ing In Truth makes us free.
The joy of the know - ing That Truth makes us free. A-men.

The Lord's My Shepherd 31

Psalm 23, Scottish Psalter, 1650
Based on Francis Rous and Others

EVAN
William H. Havergal, 1846

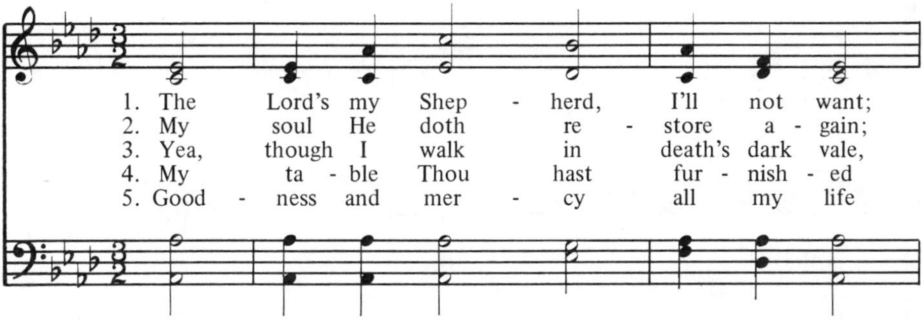

1. The Lord's my Shep - herd, I'll not want;
2. My soul He doth re - store a - gain;
3. Yea, though I walk in death's dark vale,
4. My ta - ble Thou hast fur - nish - ed
5. Good - ness and mer - cy all my life

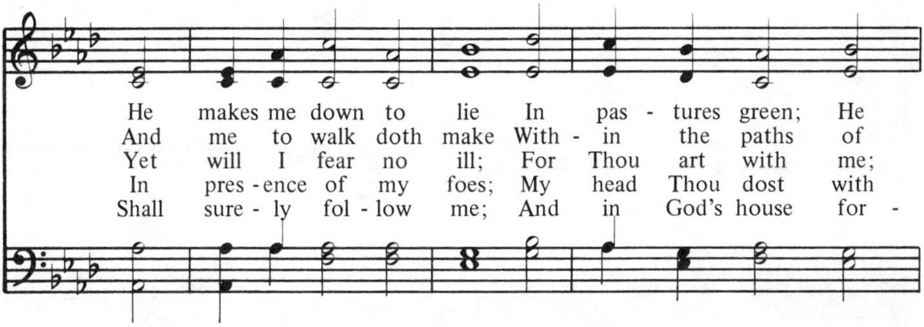

He makes me down to lie In pas - tures green; He
And me to walk doth make With - in the paths of
Yet will I fear no ill; For Thou art with me;
In pres - ence of my foes; My head Thou dost with
Shall sure - ly fol - low me; And in God's house for -

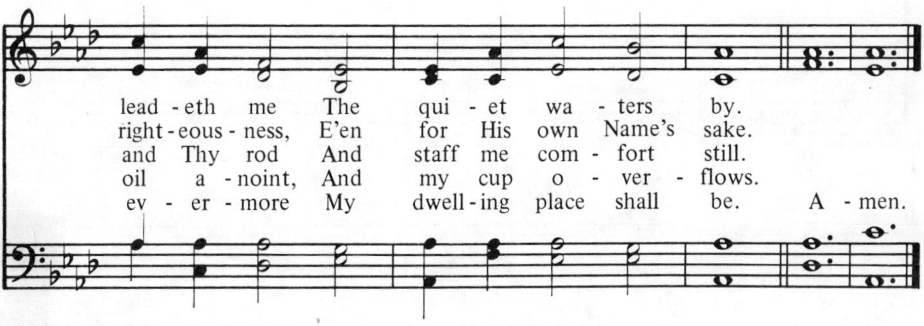

lead - eth me The qui - et wa - ters by.
right - eous - ness, E'en for His own Name's sake.
and Thy rod And staff me com - fort still.
oil a - noint, And my cup o - ver - flows.
ev - er - more My dwell - ing place shall be. A - men.

Temper My Spirit, O Lord

AGNI

Jean Starr Untermeyer, 1921

Grace Wilbur Conant, 1927

1. Tem - per my spir - it, O Lord, And burn out its al - loy;
2. Tem - per my spir - it, O Lord, Keep it long in the fire;
Make it a pli-ant steel for Thy wield-ing, Not a clum-sy toy;
Make it one with the flame, let it share that Up - reach-ing de - sire.
A blunt iron thing in my hands, That blun - der and de - stroy.
Grasp it, Thy - self, O my God, Swing it straight - er and high - er!

Words from "Love and Need." Used by permission of Michel Farano, literary executor of the estate of Jean Starr Untermeyer. Slightly altered for this hymnal. Music by permission of Fleming H. Revell Co., Old Tappan, N. J.

Tem - per my spir-it, O Lord, Tem - per my spir-it, O Lord.
Tem - per my spir-it, O Lord, Tem - per my spir-it, O Lord. A - men.
Dear Lord and Father of Mankind
33
REST
John G. Whittier, alt.
Frederick C. Maker
1. Dear Lord and Fa - ther of man-kind, For - give our fool - ish ways;
2. Breathe through the pulse of our de - sire Thy cool - ness and thy balm;
3. Drop thy still dews of qui - et - ness 'Til our wild striv - ings cease;
Re - clothe us in our right - ful mind, 'Til in our lives thy
With - in our con - scious - ness in - spire, Speak through the earth-quake,
Take from our souls the strain and stress 'Til we with or - dered
truth we find, And with new rev - 'rence, praise.
wind and fire, O still small voice of calm.
lives ex - press The beau - ty of thy peace.

34 A Thousand Ways

Della A. Leitner

AMESBURY
Uzziah C. Burnap

1. God has a thou-sand ways to bring My per-fect good to me;
2. Mine is the task to wait in faith, And as I wait to do

I need not des - ig - nate or say What chan - nel it shall be.
What lies at hand with will - ing-ness And trust His prom-ise true.

A glad sur - prise may be in store; New paths may o - pen wide;
A thou-sand ways—yes, these and more Can man - i - fest, and so

New tho'ts may come and new i - deas His boun-ty to pro - vide.
Why should I doubt? Why should I fear? My part is but to know. A-men.

Through the Love of God, Our Father 35

AR HYD Y NOS
Trad. Welsh Melody
Harm. by L. O. Emerson

Mary B. Peters, adapted

1. Through the love of God, our Fa - ther, All will be well;
2. Though we pass through trib - u - la - tion, All will be well;
3. See - ing now a bright to - mor - row, All will be well;
Free and change-less is his fa - vor, And all is well;
Life ful - fills each ex - pec - ta - tion, And all is well;
Faith can sing through days of sor - row, And all is well;
Glo - rious - ly his love re - vealed us, Pa - tient - ly his truth has healed us,
While his truth we are ap - ply - ing, And up - on his love re - ly - ing,
Joy - ful - ly in mind con - fid - ing, Ev - er find-ing God a - bid - ing,
Ev - er shall his pow - er shield us, And all is well.
God is ev - ery need sup - ply - ing, And all is well.
His re - spon - sive spir - it guid - ing, All now is well. A-men.

36 Thou, Christ of God, Indwelling

Thos. L. McClellan

MUNICH
"Gesangbuch", Meiningen, 1693
Harm. by Felix Mendelssohn

1. Thou, Christ of God, in - dwell - ing, Each man's own guid - ing star,
2. Thou, Christ of God, po - ten - tial, In ev - ery man the heart,
3. Thou, Christ of God, in - spir - ing, Be Thou with - in each prayer,

That Je - sus knew ex - cell - ing And taught both near and far;
The spir - it and es - sen - tial, That knows it knows Thou art;
That we from Thee ac - quir - ing, Shall in true glo - ry share;

We praise the mas - ter's in - sight, He lived, ex - pressed and proved
In all Thou art in - her - ent, Each man Thy im - aged son,
Thy wis - dom in us flow - ing, We shall through faith per - ceive,

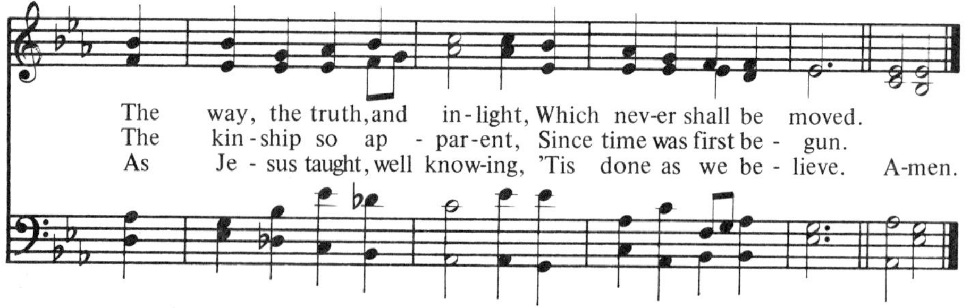
The way, the truth, and in - light, Which nev - er shall be moved.
The kin - ship so ap - par - ent, Since time was first be - gun.
As Je - sus taught, well know - ing, 'Tis done as we be - lieve. A - men.

O Christ, Thou Great Example Known 37

ST. LEONARD (HILES)
Henry Hiles, 1867

Thos. L. McClellan

1. O Christ, thou great ex - am - ple known In whom God's pow'r held sway,
2. Thou knew - est that the Fath - er is In - her - ent in man - kind;
3. O Christ, thy un - der - stand - ing shows The way, the truth, the light;
Re - new - ing heart and mind of man In love's tri - um - phant way,
And as thou knew thy God with - in, So shall all know and find;
Thy wis - dom ev - er beam - ing clear With - in the dark - est night;
Thou knew - est that mere suf - fer - ing It - self has lit - tle worth,
For mind and spir - it in all men Ex - pand e - ter - nal - ly,
Be - liev - ing in one's God and self, Man's joy finds full re - lease,
But from with - in one's con - scious - ness Man finds re - deem - ing birth.
Cre - a - tion's great re - sur - gence to New glo - ries yet to be.
And love of neigh - bor as one's self Is man's a - bun - dant peace. A - men.

I Have a Ship

KINGSFOLD
Melody coll. Lucy Broadwood
Arr. & harm. R. Vaughan Williams

Thos. L. McClellan

1. I have a ship in which God dwells, The bal - last is set deep;
2. And to my God I'll grate - ful be, Though I be tossed a - bout;
3. And though my ship seems all my own, It real - ly is not mine;
And though the winds bring heav - y swells, My ship will stead - y keep;
For He the stars has giv - en me, To read and nev - er doubt;
The build - er who to all is known, Cre - a - ted the de - sign;
And should I put my ship to sea, And winds be - come a gale,
And though the storm my sails may rip, I'll chart my course a - new;
And so to Him I'll sing my praise, And though I trav - el wide,
Still God is with me con-stant - ly, What - ev - er may as - sail.
I'll mend the sails that move my ship, And new hor - i - zons view.
My ship I'll sail through all my days With un - as - sum - ing pride. A - men.

I Am the Shepherd 39

FOREST GREEN

Laura Helser, paraphrased
by Thos. L. McClellan

English Melody, Coll., Adapted, &
Arr. by Ralph Vaughan Williams, 1906

1. I am the shep-herd of my tho'ts, Though far a - way they roam, Each
2. I am the shep-herd of my tho'ts, The guard - ian of my sheep, And
3. I am the shep-herd of my tho'ts, To tend with lov - ing care, And

thought a - stray I'll turn and guide, 'Til each a - gain is home; And
yet I have a shep-herd too, In whom my trust I keep; My
as they feed on God's own gifts, Their wool grows full and fair; I

though they roam o'er hill and dale, And scam-per to and fro, I'll
Shep - herd's ways are safe and sure, With love his arms ex - tend To
am the mas - ter of my flock, And nour-ished by God's grace, My

watch and tend them ev - ery one, As they to full-ness grow.
guide my tho'ts to pas-tures green, In ev - ery vale I wend.
thots shall grow in truth and strength, And reach their right-ful place.

40 O Thou Great and Mighty Father

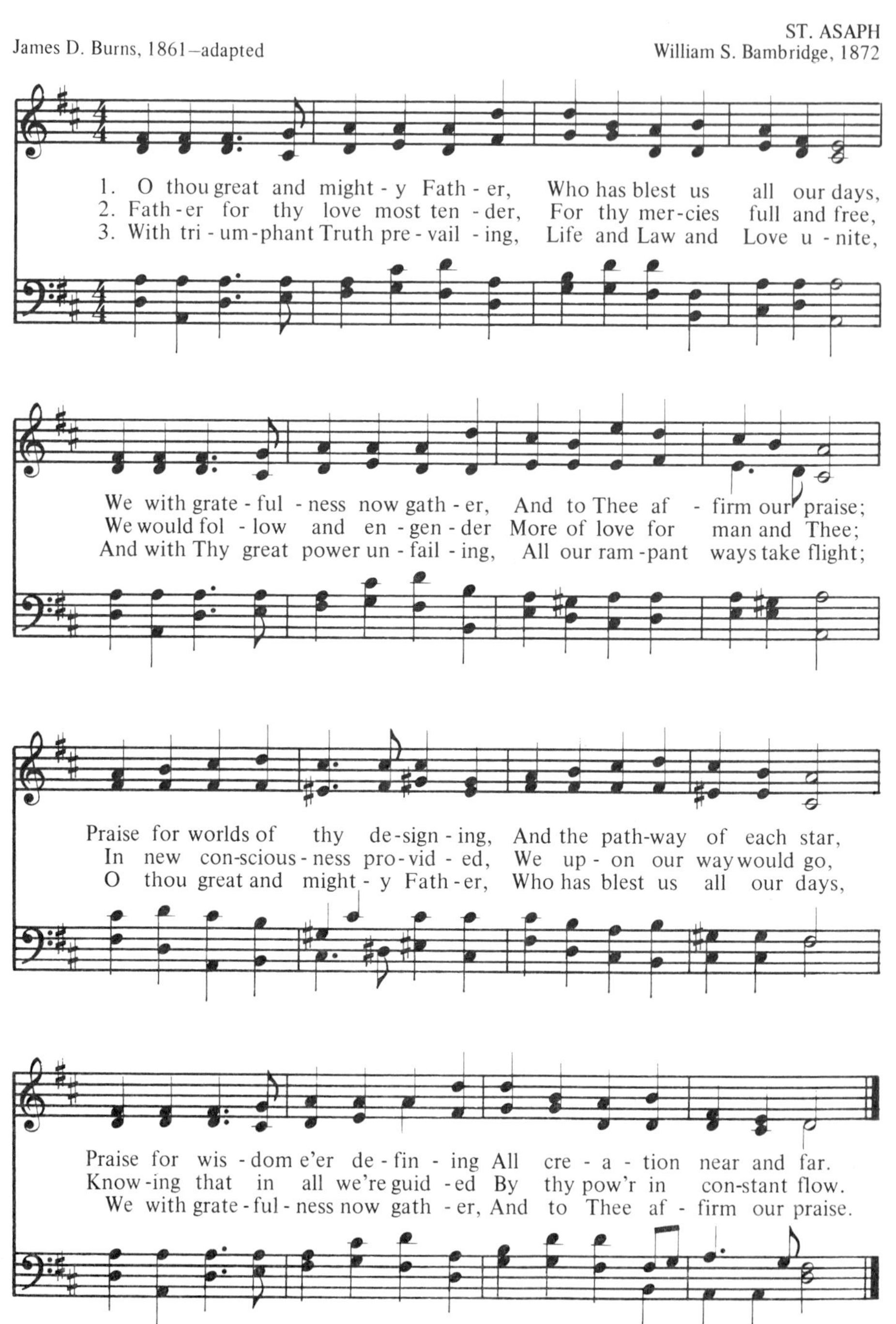
ST. ASAPH
James D. Burns, 1861–adapted
William S. Bambridge, 1872
1. O thou great and might - y Fath - er, Who has blest us all our days,
2. Fath - er for thy love most ten - der, For thy mer - cies full and free,
3. With tri - um - phant Truth pre - vail - ing, Life and Law and Love u - nite,
We with grate - ful - ness now gath - er, And to Thee af - firm our praise;
We would fol - low and en - gen - der More of love for man and Thee;
And with Thy great power un - fail - ing, All our ram - pant ways take flight;
Praise for worlds of thy de - sign - ing, And the path - way of each star,
In new con - scious - ness pro - vid - ed, We up - on our way would go,
O thou great and might - y Fath - er, Who has blest us all our days,
Praise for wis - dom e'er de - fin - ing All cre - a - tion near and far.
Know - ing that in all we're guid - ed By thy pow'r in con - stant flow.
We with grate - ful - ness now gath - er, And to Thee af - firm our praise.

Guide Me, O Thou Living Presence 41

CWM RHONDDA
Welsh Hymn Melody
John Hughes

William Williams, adapted

1. Guide me, O Thou Liv - ing Pres - ence When I tread on
2. Guide me with thy light and wis - dom, Bid my wan - der -
3. Op - en now the crys - tal foun - tain, Whence the heal - ing
bar - ren land; With thy love and truth sus - tain - ing, guide me with thy
ings sub - side; Lead me to the land a - bun - dant, Be thou e'er my
stream doth flow; While new con - scious-ness with - in me Leads me on my
pow'r - ful hand; Thou art might - y, guid - ing right - ly,
con - stant guide; Ev - er reign - ing, nev - er wan - ing,
jour - ney through; In me liv - ing, ev - er giv - ing,
Be thou still my strength and shield, Be thou still my strength and shield.
As thou show-est let me find, As thou show-est, let me find.
Joy - ful - ly thy praise I sing, Joy - ful - ly thy praise I sing. A-men.

42 Love Divine, All Love Excelling

Based on Charles Wesley, 1747

BEECHER
John Zundel, 1870

1. Love di - vine, all love ex - cel - ling, Joys of heav'n, in earth a - bound! We re - main Thy ho - ly dwell - ing, All Thy faith - ful mer - cies crown. Love di - vine is Life's ex - press - ion, Pure, un - bound - ed love we see;
2. Praise to Thee, O great Cre - a - tor! Praise be Thine from ev - 'ry tongue; O, let ev - 'ry liv - ing crea - ture Join the u - ni - ver - sal song! Spir - it, Source of all our be - ing, Free, e - ter - nal life is Thine:
3. Rich - es come of Thee, and hon - or, Pow'r and might to Thee be - long; Thine it is to make us pros - per, On - ly Thine to make us strong. Lord to Thee, Thou God of mer - cy, Hymns of grat - i - tude we raise;

Verses 2 and 3 from the "Unity Hymnal".

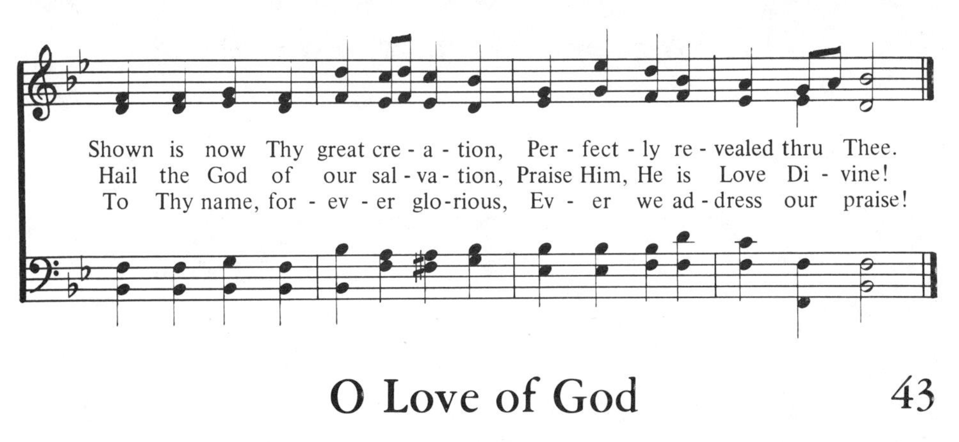
Shown is now Thy great cre - a - tion, Per - fect - ly re - vealed thru Thee.
Hail the God of our sal - va - tion, Praise Him, He is Love Di - vine!
To Thy name, for - ev - er glo - rious, Ev - er we ad - dress our praise!

O Love of God

43

BELOIT

Horatius Bonar, 1861, alt.

Carl G. Reissiger

1. O Love of God, how strong and true! E - ter - nal
2. O Love of God, how deep and great! Far deep - er
3. O Love of God, our shield and stay! Thru all the

and yet ev - er new; Un - com - pre - hend - ed
than man's deep - est hate; Self - fed, self - kin - dled
per - ils of our way; E - ter - nal Love, in

and un - bought, Be - yond all knowl - edge and all thought.
like the light, E - ter - nal, change - less, in - fi - nite.
Thee we rest, For - ev - er sure, for - ev - er - blest.

44 The Heavens Declare Thy Glory

Thomas R. Birks, alt.

FAR-OFF LANDS
Melody of the Bohemian Brethren,
in Hemmets Koral Bok,
Arr. Winfred Douglas, 1943

1. The heav'ns de-clare thy glo-ry, The fir-ma-ment thy power;
2. The sun with roy-al splen-dor Goes forth to chant thy praise;
3. All heaven on high re-joic-es To do its Mak-er's will;

Day un-to day the sto-ry Re-peats from hour to hour;
The moon-beams soft and ten-der Their gen-tler an-them raise;
And stars with sol-emn voic-es Re-sound thy prais-es still;

Night un-to night re-ply-ing, Pro-claims in ev-ery land,
O'er ev-ery tribe and na-tion The vi-bran-cy is poured,
So let my whole be-hav-ior, Thoughts, words, and ac-tions be,

O Lord, with voice un-dy-ing, The won-ders of thy hand.
The song of all cre-a-tion To Thee, cre-a-tion's Lord.
O Lord, my Strength, my Sav-ior, One cease-less song to Thee. A-men.

From Glory unto Glory

Frances R. Havergal, adapted

ALFORD
John B. Dykes

1. From glo - ry un - to glo - ry, Be this our joy - ous song;
2. The full - ness of His bless-ing En - com - pass - es our way;
3. From glo - ry un - to glo - ry, What great things He has done,
From glo - ry un - to glo - ry, 'Tis Love that leads us on;
The full - ness of His prom - ise Crowns ev - 'ry dawn-ing day;
What won - ders He has shown us, What tri - umphs Love has won!
As wid - er yet and wid - er, The ris - ing splen - dors glow,
The full - ness of His glo - ry Is shin - ing from a - bove,
From glo - ry un - to glo - ry, From strength to strength we go,
What wis - dom is re - vealed to us, What free - dom we may know!
While more and more we learn to know The full - ness of His love.
While grace for grace a - bun - dant - ly Does from His full-ness flow.

46 In Truth Be Thy Trust

LYONS
H. Edward Mills
William Gardiner's Sacred Melodies, 1815
1. In Truth be thy trust, in Love thy de - light; Be
2. Stand thou and de - clare thy per-fect re - lease; And
3. Let Truth be thy sword, and Love be thy shield. The
joy - ful and just, have faith in the right. With -
claim thy full share of health and of peace. Thy
pow'r of the land shall thus be re - vealed. So
in thee there reign - eth a King on His throne, And
bold ex - pec - ta - tion ful - fill - ment shall find, When
might - y so ten - der, so true to the end, Thy
ev - er main - tain - eth thy pow - er by His own.
faith and e - la - tion have gird - ed thy mind.
Mak - er, De - fend - er and In - fin - ite Friend.

Jesus, May All Men Awaken 47

FABEN

Henry F. Lyte, adapted

John H. Willcox

1. Je - sus, may all men a - wak - en, And be - lieve like un - to thee;
2. Je - sus, thou hast shown the glo - ry, And the maj - es - ty of life;
May thy truth be not for - sak - en, Thou who lived to make men free;
Shown in par - a - ble and sto - ry Love shall o - ver-come all strife;
May we nour - ish to fru - i - tion The pure seeds that thou hast sown;
May we more of truth be learn - ing, And the Fa - ther's in - ward pow'r,
And re - spon - sive to our mis - sion, Har - vest love more ful - ly grown.
While we're thought - ful - ly dis - cern - ing The po - ten - tial of each hour.

48 We Build a New Tomorrow

Vs. 1 & 2 Anonymous
Vs. 3 Alvin D. St. John

WEBB
George J. Webb, 1837

1. We build a new to - mor - row, We draw the pat - tern clear,
2. We clear the heart of ha - tred, We clear the mind of fear;
3. What - ev - er things are love - ly, What - ev - er - things are true,
We make our plans with wis - dom, For Mind is ev - er here.
We speak no word of cen - sure Of all we see or hear.
What - ev - er things are no - ble, We bring them in - to view.
Our think - ing makes our fu - ture, Our ac - tions pave the way;
With Love to guard and guide us, With Mind to light the way,
The cor - ner - stone of heav - en For guid - ing lines we lay;
We build a new to - mor - row, On pat-terns formed to - day.
We build a new to - mor - row, On sites we clear to - day.
We build a new to - mor - row, With love and joy to - day.

Verse 3 used by permission of author.

The Morn of Truth Is Breaking 49

MENDEBRAS
Old German Melody
Arr. by Lowell Mason

Mary E. Butters, alt.

1. The morn of Truth is break - ing; Ten thou-sand notes of love
2. O reign in ev - ery house-hold, And where there's one soul sad,
3. O Thou, most peace-ful Pres - ence, Make glad our on-ward way,
From tune-ful souls are wak - ing, To swell the songs a - bove.
Come as a ra - diant an - gel, A light to make it glad.
With beams of liv - ing love -light Chase all things false a - way.
Come raise a glo - rious an - them Far o - ver hill and plain,
O Truth, shine on in splen - dor, Dis - pel all shades of gloom,
Thou art the Light of heav - en In ev - ery quest and goal,
For Truth in ra - diant splen-dor Has come on earth to reign.
And where there seems a des - ert, The rose shall burst in bloom.
Shine Thou, O Truth, in splen-dor, Glow Thou in ev - ery soul.

From "Unity Song Selections". Words slightly altered for this hymnal.

50 Abide with Me

H. Edward Mills
EVENTIDE
Wm. H. Monk
1. A - bide with me, thou con - scious - ness of God;
2. Brief in their lus - tre, things of time and sense
3. Rich are the rap - tures of the know - ing soul.
Lest to my - self I seem but clay or clod.
Rule for a day, then pass ob - scure - ly hence.
Light, life and love the path - way and the goal.
Made in God's im - age, I di - vine must be;
I still re - main, heir of e - ter - ni - ty;
More deep each day be my tran - quil - i - ty;
Thou pure God con - scious-ness, A - bide with me.
Thou con-scious - ness of God, A - bide with me.
Thou con-scious - ness of God, A - bide with me.

Breathe on Me, Breath of God 51

TRENTHAM
Edwin Hatch, adapted
Robert Jackson
1. Breathe on me, Breath of God, Make me a - wake, a - ware, That I may
2. Breathe on me, Breath of God, Un - til my life is free, Un - til my
3. Breathe on me, Breath of God, 'Til all my thoughts are thine, 'Til all this
4. Breathe on me, Breath of God, 'Til truth is ful - ly sown, 'Til in thy
find thy love, which waits For me to know and share.
heart and mind, and will Re - spond as one with Thee.
earth-ly part of me Glows with thy fire di - vine.
spir - it in - fin - ite I know as I am known. A - men.
Word adaptation © 1972 Thos. L. McClellan. Used by permission.
Holy Spirit, Truth Divine
52
MERCY
Samuel Longfellow, 1864
Adapted
Louis M. Gottschalk, 1867
1. Ho - ly Spir - it, Truth di - vine, Dawn up - on this soul of mine;
2. Ho - ly Spir - it, Love di - vine, Glow with - in this heart of mine;
3. Ho - ly Spir - it, Strength di - vine, Fill and nerve this will of mine;
4. Ho - ly Spir - it, Source di - vine, In - ward Be - ing Di - vine - ly mine;
Word of God, and in - ward Light, Wake my know-ing, clear my sight.
Light the path-way and in - spire, Kin-dle ev - 'ry high de - sire.
By Thee shall I e'er en - dure, Nev-er want-ing, ev - er sure.
Thy true glo - ry may I see, Now and through e - ter - ni - ty. A - men.

Word adaptation © 1972 Thos. L. McClellan. Used by permission.

I Hear Thy Voice

Marion Franklin Ham

Thos. L. McClellan

1. I hear thy voice, with - in the si - lence speak - ing;
2. In sor - row's hour, when frown-ing storm clouds hide Thee,
3. When e - vil reigns, life's dark - er depths re - veal - ing,
A - bove earth's din it ris - es calm and clear;
And faith can see no friend - ly stars a - bove,
And all the good seems sad - ly marred by wrong,
What - ev - er goal my way - ward will is seek - ing,
Still through the gloom, Thy words of com-fort guide me,
A - midst the dis - cord, like sweet mu - sic steal - ing,
Its whis-pered mes-sage tells me Thou art near.
And I find light and shel-ter in Thy love.
Thy voice a - bid - ing, fills my soul with song.

Thou Wilt Keep Him in Perfect Peace 54

Isaiah 26: 3
Vivian Kretz Amsler

Vivian Kretz Amsler

1. Thou wilt keep him in per - fect peace Whose mind is stayed on Thee;
2. Thou wilt keep him in per - fect peace Whose mind is stayed on Thee;
All the glo-ries of his love be - hold, And feel all tur - moils cease;
With an- tic- i - pa- tion now be - lieve, Let high- er thots now reign;
Let thy un - der - stand-ing trust en - fold, And find a full re - lease;
With a - ware-ness in thy heart re - ceive, Let joy be thy re - frain;
Thou wilt keep him in per - fect peace Whose mind is stayed on Thee.
Thou wilt keep him in per - fect peace Whose mind is stayed on Thee.

55 Open My Eyes that I May See

Clara H. Scott
Clara H. Scott
1. O - pen my eyes, that I may see, Glimp-ses of truth Thou hast for me;
2. O - pen my ears, that I may hear Voic - es of truth Thou send - est clear;
3. O - pen my mouth and let me bear Glad - ly the warm truth ev - ery-where;
*4. My mind is o - pen, now I see Full - ness of truth Thou hast for me;
Place in my hands the won - der - ful key That shall un - clasp, and set me free.
And while the wave - notes fall on my ear, Ev - ery-thing false will dis - ap - pear.
O - pen my heart and let me pre - pare Love with Thy chil - dren thus to share.
And in my soul that won - der - ful key O - pens the door to set me free.
Si - lent - ly now I wait for Thee, Read - y, my God, Thy will to see;
Si - lent - ly now I wait for Thee, Read - y, my God, Thy will to see;
Si - lent - ly now I wait for Thee, Read - y, my God, Thy will to see;
Joy - ous - ly now I am with Thee, Let - ting Thy light il - lu - mine me,
O - pen my eyes, il - lu - mine me, Spir - it di - vine!
O - pen my ears, il - lu - mine me, Spir - it di - vine!
O - pen my heart, il - lu - mine me, Spir - it di - vine!
For in my heart Thy will I see, Spir - it di - vine! A - men.

* Fourth verse added for this hymnal.

Spirit of God

56

Rosa Horn Rose
Rosa Horn Rose
1. Spir - it of Life e - ter - nal, Spir - it of Life un - seen,
2. Spir - it of Life e - ter - nal, Joy to my soul thou art,
Thou art the Source of Pow - er, Per-fect, com-plete, se - rene;
Ev - er sus - tain - ing, strength - 'ning, The will-ing, seek-ing heart.
Spir - it of God with - in me, Wise and un-fail - ing Guide,
Spir - it of God with - in me, Wait - ing thy power to give,
Thou art the Liv - ing Pres - ence, In Thee I now a - bide.
Thou art my ver - y Be - ing; In Thee I am and live.

From "Religious Science Hymnal". Used by permission of Dodd, Mead & Co.
Verse 2 added for this hymnal © 1972 Thos. L. McClellan

57 Sweet Hour of Prayer

William W. Walford, adapted
SWEET HOUR
William B. Bradbury
1. Sweet hour of prayer, sweet hour of prayer, That calls me from a
2. Sweet hour of prayer, sweet hour of prayer, The joy I feel, the
3. Sweet hour of prayer, sweet hour of prayer, That brings a qui - et,
world of care; And bids me at my Fa - ther's throne, Make
bliss I share; I know that truth in con - scious - ness A -
calm - ness there; And as I pray, re - laxed, and free, My
all my wants and wish - es known; In sea - sons of dis - tress and
waits my seek - ing soul to bless; And with an un - di - vid - ed
soul a - wakes, and seeks to be; And as new thoughts with - in me
grief, My soul has of - ten found re - lief, In new a - ware - ness
mind, God's con - stant bless - ings I will find, And so re - leas - ing
soar To realms that touch on heav - en's door, My be - ing now tran -

wait - ing there, Through thy re - turn sweet hour of prayer.
ev - ery care, I wel-come thee sweet hour of prayer.
scends des - pair, And I am blessed sweet hour of prayer. A - men.

Not So in Haste, My Heart! 58

DOLOMITE CHANT
Austrian melody

Bradford Torrey, 1875

Harm. by Joseph T. Cooper, 1877

Eb Bb7 Bb Bb7 Eb

1. Not so in haste, my heart! De - clare thy good to - day;
2. Have faith in God and wait! With pa-tience plant the seed;
3. Not so in haste, my heart! The path-way shall be clear:
4. Un - til it com - eth rest! Nor grudge the hours that roll;

Eb7 Ab Eb7 Ab Ab6 Eb

Vex not thy - self with how, Nor spec - i - fy the way.
Thy thoughts shall ac - ti - vate, And God with - in shall lead.
In qui - et will - ing - ness, The an - swer you will hear.
The feet that walk with God, Are soon - est at the goal.

Bb sus Bb7 Eb Ab Eb

A - men.

59 Ever So Wondrously

Thos. L. McClellan

Will L. Thompson

1. Ev - er so won - drous - ly, God seems to be
2. Ev - er so pa - tient - ly, God seems to be
3. Ev - er so ten - der - ly, God seems to be
Read - y my soul to in - spire; This in - ward trea - sure, a -
Read - y my mind to re - new With truth un - seal - ing, and
Add - ing his love to my heart; Calm - ing and heal - ing each
bun - dant in mea - sure, Waits to ful - fill my de - sire.
wis - dom re - veal - ing, Deep in my own con - scious view.
thought and each feel - ing, To give my life a new start.
Refrain
I know that God is there, Con - stant - ly read - y His
pow'r to share; Clear - ly, more dear - ly, God

rit.
liv - ing in me Ev - er is read - y to share.
O Mighty God, Thy Spirit One
60
BEATITUDO
Thos. L. McClellan
John B. Dykes
1. O might - y God, thy Spir - it one, Which all of
2. The es - sence of each thought un - sealed, And filled with
3. The in - spir - a - tion of each heart, Be - liev - ing
4. In each ex - pres - sion it is shown, With deep - er
space doth frame, Thy pres - ence lives with - in each
truth di - vine, The strength-'ning pow'r in men re -
and se - rene, The joy and love that men im -
clar - i - ty, We walk with Thee, and not a -
Son To glo - ri - fy thy Name.
vealed, Are im - ag - es of thine.
part, Re - flect thy life with - in.
lone, Through all e - ter - ni - ty. A - men.

61 Eternal Mind

GERALD
Mary Alice Dayton
Adapted from Louis Spohr
1. E - ter - nal Mind the Pot-ter is, And tho't th'e-ter -nal clay;
2. God could not make im - per-fect man, His mod-el in - fin - ite;
3. God's will is done; His king-dom come; The Pot-ter's work is plain;
The hand that fash-ions is di - vine, His works pass not a - way.
Un - hal-lowed tho't he could not plan, Love's work and Love must fit.
The long - ing for ex - pres - sion true Has brought the light a - gain.
Man is the no - blest work of God, His beau-ty pow'r and grace;
Life, Truth and Love the pat - tern make, Christ is the per - fect heir;
And man does stand as God's own child, The im - age of His love;
Im - mor-tal; per - fect as his Mind Re - flect-ed face to face.
The clouds of sense roll back, and show The form di-vine-ly fair.
Let glad - ness ring from ev - 'ry tongue, And heaven and earth ap - prove. A-men.

Father, to Us Thy Constant Love Revealing 62

James F. Clarke, adapted

PRAYER
Anonymous

1. Fa - ther, to us thy con - stant love re - veal - ing;
2. Let all thy good - ness by our mind be heed - ed;
In our a - ware - ness, let thy will hold claim;
Let new a - ware - ness now be - come re - vealed;
Give such a force of ho - ly thought and feel - ing
Thy pow'r, O God, can give the cleans - ing need - ed,
That we may live to glo - ri - fy thy name.
And waits for us to wa - ken and be healed. A - men.

63 Spirit of God, Awaken Now My Heart

MORECAMBE

Composite from George Croly

Frederick C. Atkinson, 1870

1. Spir - it of God, a - wak - en now my heart,
2. I ask no dream, no proph - et ec - sta - cies,
3. Teach me to feel that Thou art al - ways nigh,
Re - new my mind; through all its puls - es move;
No sud - den rend - ing of the veil of clay,
One ho - ly pas - sion fill - ing all my frame;
Stoop to my weak - ness, might - y as Thou art,
No an - gel vis - i - tant, no open - ing skies;
Teach me to check the ris - ing reb - el sigh;
Teach me to love Thee as I ought to love.
But take the dim - ness of my soul a - way.
In heart, and mind, and soul, be Thou the flame. A - men.

O Brother Man, Fold to Thy Heart 64

WELWYN
John G. Whittier
Alfred Scott-Gatty
1. O broth - er man, fold to thy heart thy broth - er;
2. Fol - low with rev - erent steps the great ex - am - ple
3. Then shall all shack - les fall, the storm - y clan - gor
Where kind - ness dwells, the peace of God is there;
Of him whose ho - ly work was do - ing good;
Of wild war mu - sic o'er the earth shall cease;
To wor - ship right - ly is to love each oth - er,
So shall the wide earth seem our Fa - ther's tem - ple,
Love shall tread out the bale - ful fire of an - ger,
Each smile a hymn, each kind - ly deed a prayer.
Each lov - ing life a psalm of grat - i - tude.
And in its ash - es plant the tree of peace. A - men.

Music used by permission of the Abbott of Downside.

65 Immortal Love

John G. Whittier, adapted

ELLACOMBE
Gesangbuch, Wirtemberg, 1784

1. Im - mor-tal Love, for - ev - er full, For - ev - er flow-ing free,
2. O Love a - wak - en us and blow The mist of doubt a - way,

For - ev - er shared, for - ev - er whole, A nev - er ebb - ing sea.
Shine out O Love Di - vine, and show The glo - ry of each day.

Though let - ters fail, and sys - tems fall, And ev - ery sym - bol wanes,
Im - mor - tal Love, for - ev - er full, For - ev - er flow - ing free,

Thy spir - it in and o - ver all E - ter - nal - ly re - mains.
For - ev - er shared, for - ev - er whole, In us for - ev - er be. A - men.

God Is Our Refuge

Adapted from Psalm 46
by Muriel Owen

Norman L. Owen

1. God is our ref - uge and our strength, A pres- ent help in trou-ble. So
2. Come and be-hold the works of God, His glo - ry is ex - alt - ed. He
there - fore we will have no fear, though all the earth should change. And
speaks and all the earth re-plies, He caus - es wars to cease. There
though the moun-tains should trem - ble, the wa - ters roar and
is a riv - er of Life whose streams make glad the hearts of
foam, "Be still and know that I am God," the Lord of Hosts is in us.
men, "Be still and know that I am God," the Lord of Hosts is in us.

67 He That Goeth Forth with Vision

IN BABILONE
Dutch Melody, ca. 1710
Harm. by Julius Röntgen

Thomas Hastings, adapted

1. He that go - eth forth with vi - sion, And on fer - tile soil he seeds,
2. Sow thy seeds, and with love nour-ish, Let not fear thy thoughts em - ploy;
Nev - er doubt - ing its fru - i - tion, Soon shall see his toil suc - ceed;
In due time the seeds will flour-ish, Thou shalt reap the fruits of joy;
Show-ers of rain will fall from heav-en, Then the cheer-ing sun will shine;
Lo, the scene of ver-dure bright-'ning, See the new - born growth ap - pear;
So shall plen-teous fruit be giv - en, Through an in - flu-ence all di - vine.
Sing thy praise, the fields are white-ning, Har - vest time a - gain is here.

Freedom

Thos. L. McClellan | Thos. L. McClellan

1. You have seen the for - ests and the hills rav-aged by the ways of men;
2. O ring out ye bells of lib - er - ty, far a - cross the noise and din,
3. Then shall all men live and tru - ly love in all lands from pole to pole,
Do you won-der wheth - er lakes and streams will be crys - tal clear a - gain.
That each man may know his free - dom ends where his broth-er's rights be - gin.
With a dis - ci - plined in - teg - ri - ty fill - ing heart and mind and soul.
You have seen the smoke-filled at - mos-phere, and have heard the ram-pant roar;
O re - sound ye bells of lib - er - ty, that all men may ful - ly hear,
And the glo - ry of true lib - er - ty, shall re - flect in the new dawn,
Do you know how great this world could be, if it were de - filed no more.
And shall feel the deep-er vi - bran - cy of your chimes that ring so clear.
When all men shall live in broth - er - hood and de - file - ment shall be gone.

69 O Thou, Whose Power

Boethius, ca. 475-525
Trans. by Samuel Johnson, 1750-alt.

ELLERS
Edward J. Hopkins

1. O Thou, whose power o'er mov - ing worlds pre - sides,
2. Through thee a - lone we calm - ly meet each test
Whose voice cre - a - ted, and whose wis - dom guides,
With con - fi - dence re - gained in si - lent rest;
With - in each soul in ra - diant splen - dor shine,
From thee, great God, we spring, to thee we tend:
And cheer the cloud - ed mind with light di - vine.
Path, mo - tive, guide, o - rig - i - nal, and end.
A - men.

Day Is Dying in the West

CHAUTAUQUA

Mary A. Lathbury, 1877, adapted

William F. Sherwin, 1877

1. Day is dying in the west, Heaven is touching earth with rest; Reassuring, as the night Sets her evening lamps alight Through all the sky.

2. While the deep'ning shadows fall, Heart of love enfolding all; Giving peace so wondrously, Essence of reality We feel Thee nigh.

3. Source of spirit's strength'ning powers, In the temple that is ours; E'er responding to our thought, With the blessings love has wrought Our hearts reply.

Refrain

Holy, Holy, Holy, Lord God of Hosts! All the universe is thine, Whole, complete, by thy design, O Lord most high! Amen.

Music from the Chautauqua Institution, N. Y.

71 Awakening Chorus

Charlotte G. Homer, alt.

Chas. H. Gabriel

C Cdim C
1. A-wake! A-wake! a - wake! a-wake! and sing the bless - ed sto - ry;
2. Ring out! Ring out! ring out! ring out! O bells of joy and glad - ness!
G G7 Gdim G7
A - wake! A-wake! a - wake! a-wake! and let your song of praise a - rise; A -
Re - peat, Re-peat, re - peat re-peat a - new the sto - ry o'er a - gain, Till
C Cdim C G
wake! a-wake! a - wake! a-wake! the earth is full of glo - ry, And light And light is
all Till all the earth the earth shall lose its weight of sad - ness, And shout And shout a
D7 G Male voices in unison C
beam - ing is beam-ing from the ra-diant skies; The rocks and rills, the vales and
new a-new the glo - ri - ous re - frain; The Light and Law of God with -
Cdim C D7
hills re-sound with glad - ness, All na ture joins to sing the tri - umph
in man-kind is reign - ing, Let all now join to sing the tri - umph

G G7 D7 G7 C F C F C
song. The Law of Good pre - vails and fear is back-ward hurled!
fear is back-ward hurled!
Gdim G Cm A7 Dm Gdim G7
Re - joice, re - joice! Lift heart and voice; The Law pre - vails!
C F C F C Am
Pro - claim this love and pow'r to all the world, And let the
pow'r to all the world, And let the
Ab7 C G7 C
earth u - nite in glo - rious song! The Law pre - vails!
whole-wide earth u - nite in glo - rious song! The Law of Good for-e'er pre - vails!
G7 C
Re - joice! re - joice! re - joice! The Law pre - vails!
Re - joice! re-joice! re-joice!

72 I Praise the Wealth of God

Angela Morgan
Ada Mitchell
1. I praise the wealth of God; His lav - ish good I sing;
2. I sing the wealth of God, It stays not in the sod,
3. The floor I dai - ly tread, The roof a - bove my head,
4. O blind and woe - be - gone, This earth is now His throne!
It flash - es from the bar - ren twig And shines in ev - 'ry - thing.
Nor dwells a - lone in sea and air; Its gold is ev - 'ry - where.
The walls I touch with star - tled sight Are shim-mer-ing with light.
Give up your grief Your voic - es raise And praise, and praise, and praise.
Chorus
I sing, I sing, I sing, My joy shall know no bound,
His glo - ry, like a daz - zling ray il - lu - mi - nates the ground.

Poem from *Whirlwind Visions* by Angela Morgan, used by permission.
From "Religious Science Hymnal". Used by permission of Dodd, Mead & Co.

God Is the Source

ASSURANCE
Thos. L. McClellan
Phoebe P. Knapp
1. God is the source of all of our good, Through Him we know more of
2. Look now with-in to your en-ti-ty, Heir to God's bless-ings a-
3. As high-er thoughts take form in the soul, They make Life's bless-ings so
truth un-der-stood; In-fin-ite Spir-it, in all man-kind,
bun-dant-ly free; Love and true wis-dom in each new age,
won-drous-ly whole; Be still and know, and let tur-moils cease,
Kin-dred of be-ing, es-sence of mind.
Pro-vides each one with God's her-it-age.
End-less as-sur-ance to joy and peace.
Refrain
God has pro-vid-ed life with a
song, And we can sing it all the day long; God has pro-vid-ed
life's har-mo-ny, Sing in your heart, and more joy-ful be.

74 Hear the Church Bells Ringing

Thos. L. McClellan
Thos. L. McClellan
1. Hear the church bells ring - ing, All the peo - ple sing - ing; O what a glo - rious day! Seek - ing minds beam bright - er, Ev - 'ry heart grows light-er, As they pray.
2. Hear the bells re - sound - ing, Vi - bran - cy a - bound - ing; O what a glo - rious day! Clouds of doubt are clear - ing, Truth and light ap - pear-ing, As they pray.
Refrain
Love and faith in - creas - ing, In - ward ten-sions ceas - ing, Souls of men are lift - ed high, Hearts in tune give their re - ply; Life a - bun - dant ov - er - flows, For God is nigh.

It Sounds Along the Ages

William Channing Gannett
Thos. L. McClellan
1. It sounds a-long the a - ges, Soul an-swer-ing to soul;
2. From Si-nai's cliffs it ech - oes, It breathed from Bud-dha's tree;
3. It calls — and lo, new jus - tice! It speaks — and lo, new truth!
It kin - dles on the pag - es Of ev - ery Bi - ble scroll.
It charmed in Ath - ens' mar - ket, It hal-lowed Gal - i - lee.
In ev - er no - bler stat - ure, And un - ex - haust - ed youth.
The psalm - ist heard and sang it, From mar - tyr lips it broke.
The ham - mer stroke of Lu - ther, The Pil - grims' sea - side prayer,
For - ev - er on re - sound - ing, And know - ing nought of time,
And proph - et tongues out - rang it, 'Til sleep - ing na - tions woke.
The or - a - cles of Con - cord — One ho - ly word de - clare.
Man's laws but catch the mu - sic Of its e - ter - nal chime.

Words by Williams Channing Gannett (1840-1923)

76 Onward Souls Eternal

ST. GERTRUDE
Fenwick L. Holmes, 1926
Arthur S. Sullivan
1. On - ward, souls e - ter - nal Rise and walk with God; Come and tread the path - way That the saints have trod; Ev - er up - ward, on - ward, Soar to heights sub - lime, Live on Spir - it's moun - tain All the days of time!
2. On - ward, souls e - ter - nal, Link your mind with God, Join your hands in ser - vice, Spread your love a - broad. Ours the creed - less un - ion, Ours the faith su - preme, Lift - ing up the ag - es To the age - less dream.
3. On - ward, then ye peo - ple, Join our hap - py throng, Blend with ours your voic - es In the tri - umph song; Glo - ry, laud and hon - or Un - to Christ the King. This thru count - less ag - es Men and an - gels sing.

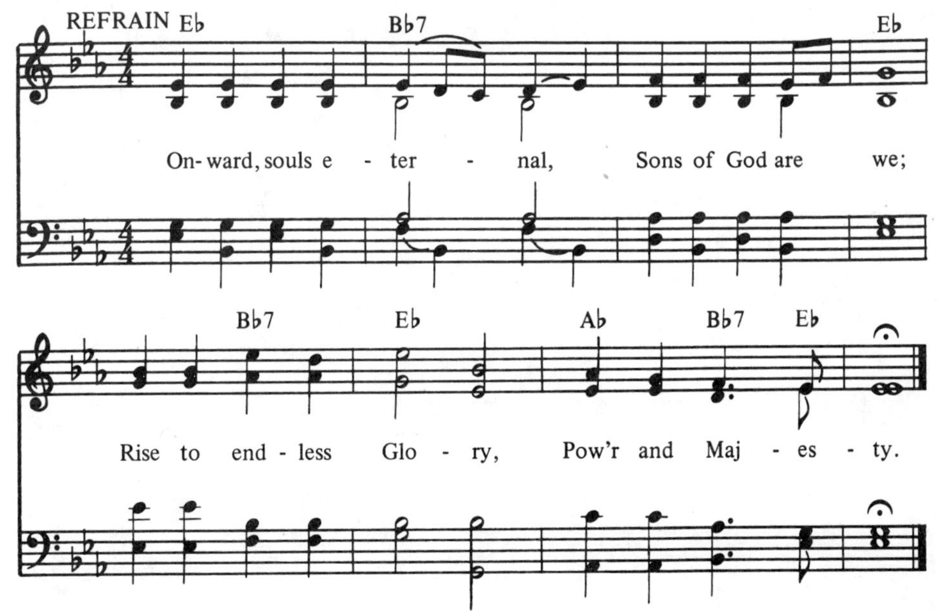
REFRAIN Eb
Bb7
Eb
On-ward, souls e - ter - nal, Sons of God are we;
Bb7
Eb
Ab
Bb7
Eb
Rise to end - less Glo - ry, Pow'r and Maj - es - ty.

No Separation

77

Albert Midlane, alt.

Early American Melody
Arr. by Edwin O. Excell

G D7 Em C G D7 G

1. "No sep-a - ra-tion!" O my soul! 'Tis God that dwells with - in, So
2. "No sep-a - ra-tion!" Linked with - in, His Spir - it now is mine; O
3. "No sep-a - ra-tion!" Pre - cious tho't! In all God will per - vade; Loved
4. "No sep-a - ra-tion!" Life nor death Things pres - ent nor to come, Can

C G Em G D7 G

close the In - fin - ite u - nites, And thus has ev - er been.
won - drous love, that thus could plan A un - ion so di - vine.
with an ev - er - last - ing love, How won-drous - ly we're made.
hide the Om - ni - pres - ence in What Spir - it has be - come.

This I Believe

Fern Brandt

Gene Graves
Arr. by Thos. L. McClellan

F C7 Ddim F C7 F7 B♭ C7
1. God is all Pow - er, His strength's with - in me (is in me);
2. A - bun - dant in me, His Love and His Law (Love and Law);
3. As Truth walks with me, O'er Life's fer - tile sod (fer - tile sod);
F C7 F C7 F
God is all Wis - dom, And through Him I see (through Him I see);
Giv - ing the an - swer To life with - out flaw (life with - out flaw);
I'm blessed in find - ing The Good - ness of God (Good - ness of God);
C7 Ddim F F7 B♭
God is Per - fec - tion, O Life I love Thee (I love Thee);
As I ac - cept Truth, And make It my own (make It my own);
Warm'd with thanks - giv - ing, This thought I re - lease (I re - lease);
F C7 F C7 F B♭ F
God is all Truth and The Truth sets me free (sets me free);
My life loves all life, And One - ness is known (One - ness is known);
Filled with God's Pres - ence, I now live in peace (live in peace);

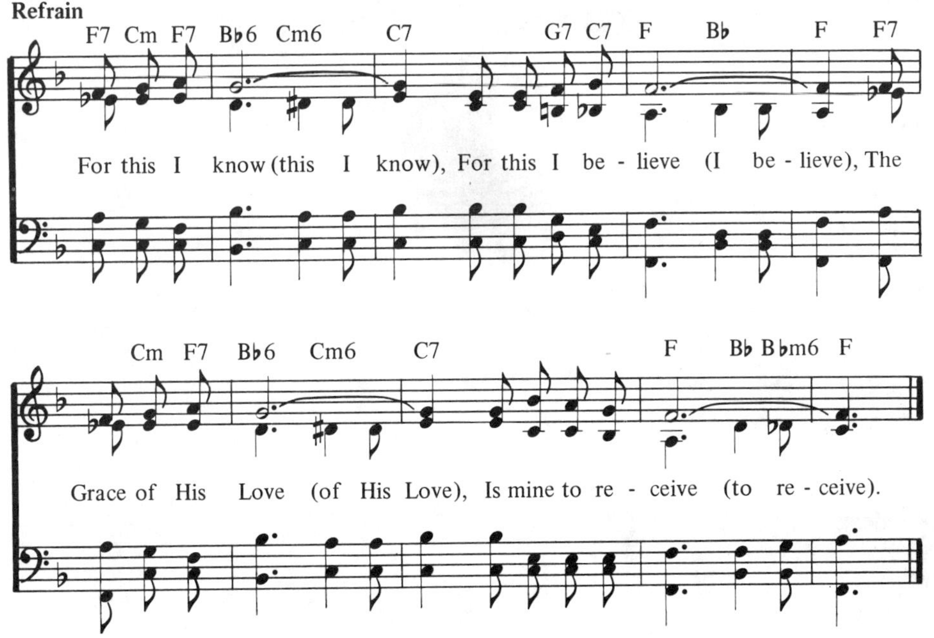

Refrain
F7 Cm F7 Bb6 Cm6 C7 G7 C7 F Bb F F7
For this I know (this I know), For this I be - lieve (I be - lieve), The
Cm F7 Bb6 Cm6 C7 F Bb Bbm6 F
Grace of His Love (of His Love), Is mine to re - ceive (to re - ceive).

Great Shepherd of All Time and Space 79

AZMON
Carl Glaser
Arr. by Lowell Mason

Thos. L. McClellan

G D G D7 Em D G D7 G D

1. Great Shep-herd of all time and space, Whose pow'r we feel and see,
2. With lov-ing heart and seek-ing mind, Thy glo-ry we shall know,
3. Great Shep-herd of each tho't and goal, From which thy glo-ry springs,
4. In faith we now re-lease all cares, And pic-ture per-fect-ness,

G C G D7 G

With-in our be-ing we em-brace Thy true re-al-i-ty.
When in our con-scious-ness re-fined, We feel thy pow-er flow.
Re-new with-in each trou-bled soul The peace thy spir-it brings.
While Love, and Life, and Truth re-pairs, And joy re-turns to bless.

80 I Love to Tell the Story

Katherine Hankey - adapted

HANKEY
William G. Fischer

G C G
1. I love to tell the sto - ry Of all that God hath wrought, Re -
2. I love to tell the sto - ry, In all of life ex - pressed, Of
3. I love to tell the sto - ry, It fills my heart with joy, Of
D7 G D7
vealed in all its glo - ry In each in - spir - ing thought; I
God's tri - um - phant glo - ry By which all men are blessed; I
wis - dom's pow'r and glo - ry A - wait - ing man's em - ploy; I
G Em B7
love to tell the sto - ry, And all its truth ex - tol: The
love to tell the sto - ry, Be - cause I know 'tis true, Of
sing the old, old sto - ry That I have loved so long, And
C G D7 G
Christ of our sal - va - tion Is God with - in man's soul.
God's e - ter - nal spir - it, In all cre - a - tion through.
feel its rhy - thm pres - ent With - in each new, new song.

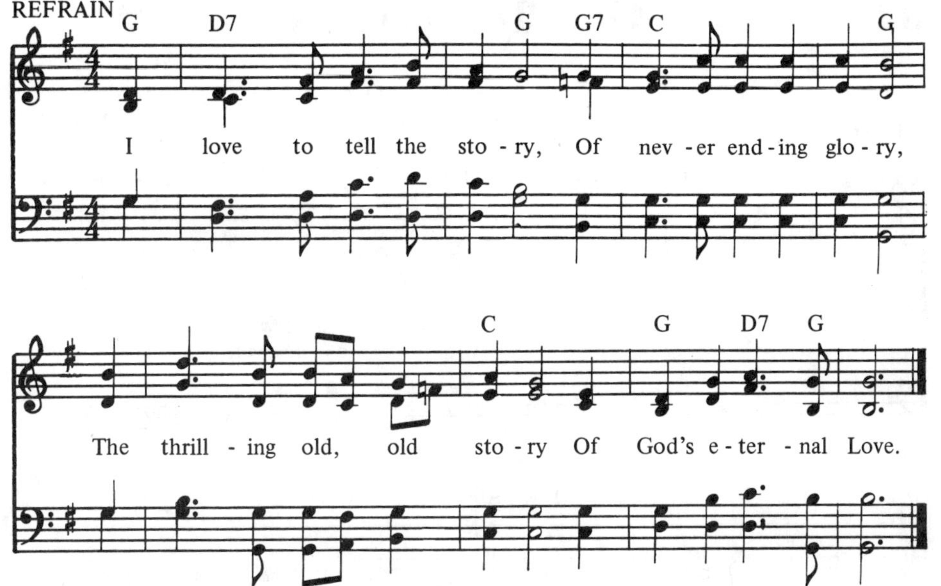
REFRAIN
G D7 G G7 C G
I love to tell the sto - ry, Of nev - er end - ing glo - ry,
C G D7 G
The thrill - ing old, old sto - ry Of God's e - ter - nal Love.

O Thou, in All Thy Might So Far 81

SERENITY

Frederick L. Hosmer, 1876

Arr. from William V. Wallace, 1856

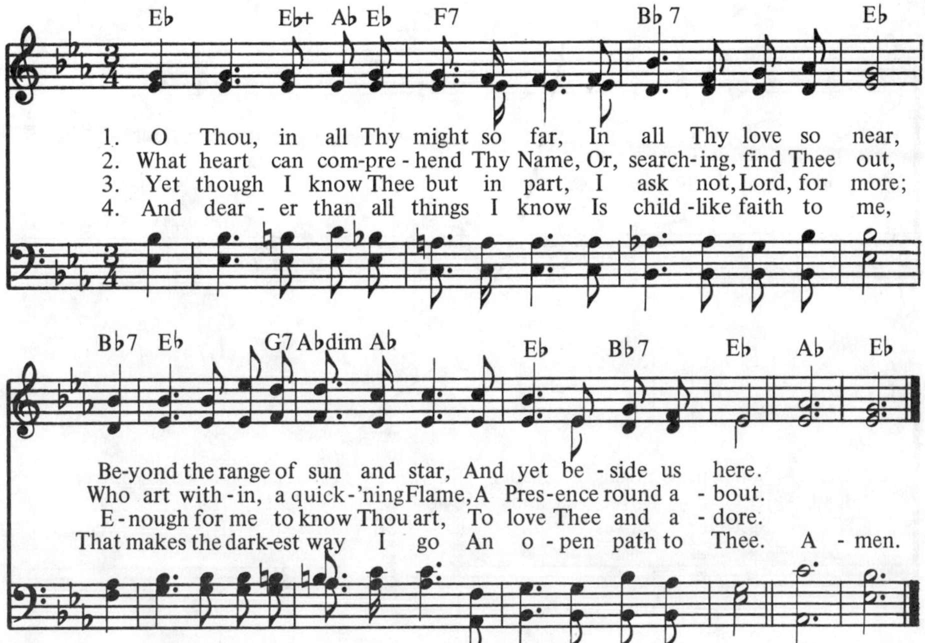

Eb Eb+ Ab Eb F7 Bb7 Eb

1. O Thou, in all Thy might so far, In all Thy love so near,
2. What heart can com-pre - hend Thy Name, Or, search-ing, find Thee out,
3. Yet though I know Thee but in part, I ask not, Lord, for more;
4. And dear - er than all things I know Is child - like faith to me,

Bb7 Eb G7 Abdim Ab Eb Bb7 Eb Ab Eb

Be-yond the range of sun and star, And yet be - side us here.
Who art with - in, a quick - 'ning Flame, A Pres - ence round a - bout.
E - nough for me to know Thou art, To love Thee and a - dore.
That makes the dark-est way I go An o - pen path to Thee. A - men.

82 God Really Lives

Elizabeth L. Owen
James H. Owen
Arr. by Michael Day
C Fdim Am Em F G G7 C
1. God real - ly lives with - in our hearts to - day;
2. We sing His praise, for in our hearts we know
3. God real - ly lives with - in our hearts to - day;
F E Am E7 Am A7 G D7 G
He knows our ev - 'ry need, He hears us pray.
God real - ly lives to - day, He loves us so.
Giv - ing true joy and peace, He is the Way.
C F F7 D G G7
He leads us on through ev - 'ry hour;
His glo - ry fills all skies a - bove,
God real - ly lives, God real - ly lives;
C F C F Dm7 C G7 C
We gain our strength through His e - ter - nal power.
Beau - ty of tree and flower re - flect His love.
His Spir - it lives in us, God real - ly lives.

Music adapted for this hymnal.

God's Constancy

HE LEADETH

Thos. L. McClellan

William B. Bradbury

C G7 C F C G7 C G
1. God's con-stan-cy, O bless-ed thought, O words of com-fort Truth has taught;
2. God's con-stan-cy is ev - 'ry - where, O heal - ing thought be - yond com - pare;
3. God's con-stan-cy in mind I know, Like heal - ing wa - ters on - ward flow;
C G7 C F C Am C G7 C
It mat - ters not the shade or hue, God's beau - ty lives to paint a - new.
It mat - ters not the tune or key, God's mu - sic lives a song to be.
It mat - ters not the time or place, God's Truth lives on with pow'r and grace.
Refrain
G7 C F C F C Am C G7
With - in my soul right now I feel A vi - brant new re - sur-gent zeal,
C G7 C F C F C Am C G7 C
Re - flect-ed there in con-scious-ness By God's e - ter - nal pow'r to bless.

84 Indwelling God

Thos. L. McClellan

MAORI MELODY
Arr. by Norman L. Owen

F Bb Bbm6 F C7 F F7
1. In - dwell-ing God, reign in my heart to - day;
2. In - dwell-ing God, be Thou my in - ward light;
3. In - dwell-ing God, my en - er - gy in - spire;
Bb E7 F G7 C7 C+
Guide and a - wak - en all my thoughts I pray;
In - still thy calm, tran - scend - ing dark - est night;
My mind re - new with wis - dom's true de - sire;
F Bb Bbm6 F C7 F F7
Re - lease in me thy ev - er pres - ent pow'r,
Make me a - ware with vi - sion grow - ing clear,
Through Thee I live sus - tained by thy de - sign;
Bb E7 F F7 D+ D7 G7 C7 F
Tem - pered by char - i - ty each pass - ing hour.
Know - ing thy strength I share, free from all fear.
Thine is the pow'r to give, ac - cep - tance mine.

I Remember

85

Carmen Moshier

Carmen Moshier

C Dm9 Em Fmaj7 C G7

I re - mem - ber, I re - mem - ber that God and I are

C C7 F G7 C A+ A7

one. There's on - ly one pow'r, there's on - ly one pow'r, that

1. D7 Dm7 G7

pow'r and I are one!

2. Dm G7 C

pow'r and I are one!

Especially arranged for this hymnal.

God's Loving Light

86

Anon.

Anon.

C Dm Em F
God's Lov-ing Light is heal-ing me now, God's Lov-ing Light is heal-ing me now,
G Am Bdim C
God's Lov-ing Light is heal - ing me now, God's Lov-ing Light is heal-ing me now;
C Bdim Am G
God's Lov-ing Light is heal - ing me now, God's Lov-ing Light is heal - ing me now,
F Em Dm C
God's Lov-ing Light is heal - ing me now, God's Lov - ing Light is heal - ing me now.

87 In the Garden

C. Austin Miles
C. Austin Miles
1. I come to the gar-den a-lone, While the dew is still on the ros-es; And the voice I hear, Fall-ing on my ear; The Son of God dis-clos-es.
2. He speaks, and the sound of His voice Is so sweet the birds hush their sing-ing, And the mel-o-dy That he gave to me, With-in my heart is ring-ing.
3. I'd stay in the gar-den with Him Tho' the night a-round me be fall-ing, But He bids me go; Thru the voice of woe, His voice to me is call-ing.
Refrain
And He walks with me, and He talks with me, And He tells me I am His own, And the joy we share as we tar-ry there, None oth-er has ev-er known.

When Twilight Shadows End the Day 88

Thos. L. McClellan
Thos. L. McClellan
Ab C C7 Fm Db Eb7 Ab
1. When twi - light shad-ows end the day, And eve-ning stars ap - pear,
2. Our mind, re - flect-ing, sees thy works With - in all time and space,
3. E - ter - nal God, thou Source of pow'r, And wis - dom's in - ward Light,
C C7 Fm Db Eb7 Ddim Eb7
We would com-mune with Thee our God, And feel thy Pres-ence near;
And mar-vels at thy gift of Life, That all cre - a - tions trace;
With grat - i - tude for ev - 'ry gift, Our song as - cends to - night;
Ab Eb7 Ab
And in this qui - et - ness, A - way from world - ly harms,
The beau - ty of each flow'r, Thy un - der - stand-ing care,
And as we con - tem - plate, We joy - ful - ly re - call
C C7 C+ Ab F7 Bb7 Eb7 Ab
There comes with - in our con - scious-ness A free-dom from a - larms.
The faith, and hope, and char - i - ty Re - veal'd with - in each pray'r.
The glo - ry of thy u - ni - verse, And Thee our All in all.

89 The Love of God in Man

Paul Martin Brunet

Paul Martin Brunet

F Dm B♭M7 C7 F Dm C C7 F Dm B♭M7 B♭6 F C
1. Deep as the o - cean, wide as the prai - ries, Is our Love for God in
Strong as the moun-tains, high as the heav - ens, Is our Love for God in
2. Come all ye peo - ple, raise up your voic - es, Sing the love of God in
Tell each oth - er, tell your broth - er, Sing the love of God in
1. F 2. F C7 F Am B♭ F
man, man. Till the glo - ry and the pow - er Shall be
man, man. Till the glo - ry and the pow - er Shall be
F F7 Dm6 G7 C G7 C F Dm B♭M7 C7 F
go - ing round the world To ev - 'ry na - tion,
known in ev - 'ry land, And all our sis - ters
F Dm C C7 F Dm B♭M7 B♭6 F C F
teach - ing sal - va - tion, Teach - ing the Love of God in man.
and all our broth - ers, Live the love of God in man.

Love

Thos. L. McClellan — Thos. L. McClellan

1. Love is like a joy - ful mel- o - dy; Love sings on in
2. Love is rev - 'rence to a Power su-preme: Love is "tun - ing
per - fect har - mo - ny. Love is giv - ing-ness with - in the soul;
in" the ra - diant beam. Love gives of It - self in quest - ing needs;
Love is lov - ing - ness com - plete and whole. Love is found in
Love is in - spir - a - tion that suc - ceeds. Love is Light out -
shar - ing; Love a - bounds in car - ing.
pour - ing; Love is Law re - stor - ing.
Love ex - press - es full and free, Love is for you and me.
Love ex - press - es full and free, Love is for you and me.

91 I Radiate the Love

Edna Mohr Dooley
Edna Mohr Dooley, ASCAP
Dm
Gm
E7
A7
1. I ra - di - ate the love that comes from deep with - in my be - ing,
2. I ra - di - ate the love that comes from deep with - in my be - ing,
Dm
Gm
Dm
Love with - in that flows ex - tend-ing far be-yond the sea,
Love that comes from God was meant for me to share with you;
A7
Dm
A7
Dm
Reach - ing out to touch an - oth - er soul in true com - mun - ion,
As I give with love a help-ing hand to ev - ery neigh- bor,
Gm7
Fdim7
A7
He's my broth - er where - so - e'er he be;
I know he will help his neigh - bor, too;

Dm Gm E7 A7
I ra - di - ate the love that comes from deep with - in my be - ing,
I ra - di - ate the love that comes from deep with - in my be - ing,
Dm Gm Dm
Love that reach - es out to hit a mark I can - not see;
Heart to heart that love goes 'round the world un-ceas - ing - ly;
A7 Dm A7 Dm
Ra - di - at - ing out to touch the world in true com - mun-ion,
Love I ra - di - ate goes 'round the world to me re - turn-ing,
Gm7 Fdim A7 Dm
Love re - turns a hun - dred-fold to me.
Love I give flows back a - gain to me.

92 They'll Know and Believe It

Peter Scholtes
Arr. by Dennis Fitzpatrick
Cong.
Fm
1. We are one in the Spir - it, We are
2. We will walk with each oth - er, We will
3. We will work with each oth - er, We will
4. All praise to the Fa - ther, From
Choir
(descant)
one in the Lord, We are
walk hand in hand, We will
work side by side, We will
whom all things come, And all
Bbm
one in the
walk with each
work with each
praise to the
Spir - it, We are
oth - er, We will
oth - er, We will
Christ - hood With - in
Fm
one in the Lord, And we
walk hand in hand, And to -
work side by side, And we'll
ev - ery Son, And all
Bbm
pray that all u - ni - ty may
geth - er we'll spread the news that
guard each man's dig - ni - ty and
praise to the Spir - it, that

Fm
Refrain
D♭
one day be re-stored.
God is in our land.
save each man's pride.
makes us one.
And they'll know and be-lieve it by our
Fm
B♭m
Fm
B♭m
Fm
love, by our love, Yes they'll know and be-lieve it by our love.
by our love.
Joy in My Heart
93
George W. Cooke
C
G7
C
1. I have the joy, joy, joy, joy, Down in my heart,
2. I have the peace that pass-eth un-der-stand-ing, Down in my heart,
3. I have the Life and Love of God with-in me, Down in my heart,
4. For there is there-fore now no con-dem-na-tion, Down in my heart,
(where)*
G7
C
Down in my heart, Down in my heart, I have the joy, joy,
Down in my heart, Down in my heart, I have the peace that pass-eth
Down in my heart, Down in my heart, I have the Life and Love of
Down in my heart, Down in my heart, For there is there-fore now no
G7
C
G7
C
joy, joy, Down in my heart, Down in my heart to stay.
un-der-stand-ing, Down in my heart, Down in my heart to stay.
God with-in me, Down in my heart, Down in my heart to stay.
con-dem-na-tion, Down in my heart, Down in my heart to stay.
(where)*

* Shout

94 God Is Growing in Me

Norman L. Owen

Guamanian Folksong
"Pues Adios Hasta Ki"
Harm. by Norman L. Owen

Bb Eb
mf 1. With man - y a tri - al and man - y a tear My
2. In warm sum-mer's eve - ning or cold win-ter's night There
Bb F7 Bb F Bb
way was once un - clear. Now trust - ing in Spir - it and
comes a thought of de - light. 'Tis in know-ing the Spir - it of
Eb Bb Gm Eb F Bb
God's change - less Law My Hope is firm and se - cure.
God dwells with - in And ra - diant-ly fills us with Light.
Refrain
F Bb Eb Bb
f God is grow-ing in me, God is flow - ing in me And my Path grows

Dedicated to the Rev. Madalyn de Grace of Riverside.

F7 Bb F C7 F Bb D7 Eb
bright - er each day. With His Light in my Soul I am gain - ing con -
C7 Bb Gm Eb F Bb
trol And my fears all van - ish a - way.

Whisper a Prayer

95

Anonymous
Vs. 3 Thos. L. McClellan

Arr. Herbert G. Tovey

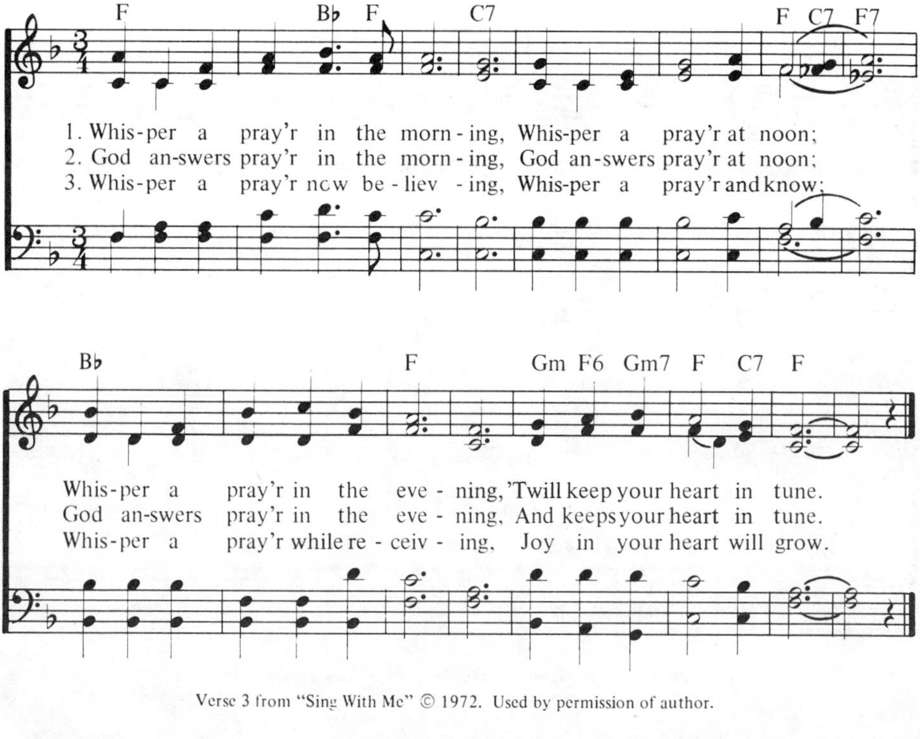

F Bb F C7 F C7 F7

1. Whis-per a pray'r in the morn - ing, Whis-per a pray'r at noon;
2. God an-swers pray'r in the morn - ing, God an-swers pray'r at noon;
3. Whis-per a pray'r now be - liev - ing, Whis-per a pray'r and know;

Bb F Gm F6 Gm7 F C7 F

Whis-per a pray'r in the eve - ning, 'Twill keep your heart in tune.
God an-swers pray'r in the eve - ning, And keeps your heart in tune.
Whis-per a pray'r while re - ceiv - ing, Joy in your heart will grow.

Walking in Spirit

Norman L. Owen

O MI QUERIDA
Arr. Norman L. Owen

D
A7
Walk-ing in Spir-it, and walk-ing in the Light, Liv-ing in
Oo
Oo
D
G
D
Spir-it and sing-ing through the night; With heart-aches and sor-rows and
Em
A7
D
E7
A
ill-ness gone a-way, God's per-fect health is mine to-day. (to-day)
D
Fdim7
O what peace and joy I feel, what hap-pi-ness is in my heart to-

Em7 A7
day! (to - day) Songs and hymns of praise are ring - ing
Em A7 D Dm A7
in my soul, 'tis more than I can say! (can say)
D D7
O the grat - i - tude I feel, the knowl-edge that my night is
G B7 Em Fdim7
turned to day! A bright light's shin-ing, yes, a
(a bright)
D E7 A7 D
new day's dawn-ing and I'm glad it's here to stay!

97 Have You Ever Seen the Beauty

BEACON HILL
Thos. L. McClellan
Harry S. Mason
1. Have you ev-er seen the beau-ty Of the ris-ing sun-light beams;
2. Have you ev-er felt the pow-er In the spring as blos-soms reign;
3. Have you ev-er known the pat-tern Of a snow-flake, none the same;
Have you ev-er seen the ra-diance In ful-fill-ment of man's dreams?
Have you ev-er felt the vig-or Of a man re-born a-gain?
Have you ev-er known the great-ness Of the God from whence man came?
Refrain
Lord God, Al-might-y, let all re-al-ize, Thou art the
es-sence of par-a-dise; One with all spir-it, and ev-er shall
be, Our heart, mind, and soul, in per-fect har-mo-ny.

Words from "Sing With Me" © 1972. Used by permission of author.
Music used by permission of Dr. Earl Marlatt.

For the Beauty of the Earth

DIX

From Folliott Sandford Pierpoint, 1864

Conrad Kocher, 1838; abridged

G D7 G D G C D7 G
1. For the beau - ty of the earth,
2. For the joy of ear and eye,
3. For the won - der of each hour
C D7 G C G D G D7 G D G
For the splen - dor of the skies, For the love which
For the heart and mind's de - light, For the mys - tic
Of the day and of the night, Hill and vale and
C D7 G C D7 G C G D G
from our birth O - ver and a - round us lies:
har - mo - ny Link - ing sense to sound and sight:
tree and flower, Sun and moon and stars of light:
D7 G D G C D7 G C G D7 G
Lord of all, to thee we raise This, our hymn of grate - ful praise.

99 Each Day I'll Live Anew

Thos. L. McClellan
Thos. L. McClellan
G B7 C D7 Bbdim G
1. Each day I'll live a - new, Lord, as though there were but one,
2. Where- ev - er I may be, Lord, my faith is born of Thee,
3. How in - fi-nite thy love, Lord, thy pres - ence now I feel;
B7 C Cm G E7 A7 Edim D7
That more of life's po - ten-tial shall be known when it is done;
And thy cre - a - tive pow-er shall my en - er - giz - ing be;
The in - ward truth Thou hast for me in con - scious-ness re - veal;
G B7 C D7 C D7 G
And though in my ex - pres - sion, some mo - ments I pro - fane,
And though I climb the moun - tain, and in its glo - ry share,
While from all bond - age free - ing, my way - ward tho'ts a - mend,
E7 A7 Adim A7 D7 G
Thy Truth in life's pro - gres - sion, time - less shall re - main.
Yet great - er is Truth's foun - tain, Lord, be - yond com - pare.
And joy shall fill my be - ing, 'til all time shall end.

When I Remember

Thos. L. McClellan
Thos. L. McClellan
Eb D Eb C+ C7
1. When my world seems cold and lone - ly, When I'm feel - ing low and blue,
2. Joy is mine and waits my bid - ding, Joy is mine in mind and soul,
Ped.
Cmi6 Bb7 Gmi Bb7 Eb Ebdim7 Eb
I re - mem - ber that God's pres - ence nev - er is a - part.
And my God with - in re - spond - ing greets my warm "Hel - lo!"
Ab Fdim Abmi Eb D D7 Eb C+ C F7
As I feel His lov - ing ra - diance, Then I re - al - ize
Friends, and Truth, and Life a - bun - dant, All are mine to find;
Bb7 Eb C+ C7 Cmi6 F7 Cmi6 Bb7 Bb+ Eb
God, my strength, is mine for - ev - er and lives with - in my heart.
And my thoughts in new ex - pres - sion set my whole heart a - glow.

101 I've Wandered

Thos. L. McClellan

Thos. L. McClellan
Arr. by Norman L. Owen

F C F F7 B♭ G
1. I've wan-dered for a long, long time, and ven - tured near and far;
2. I've searched this world, both far and wide, to find the Truth you see;
3. Now life has new per - spec-tive, and my ways are tru - ly changed;
4. I've found a Liv - ing Pres - ence that is mine to know and feel;
C7 F G7 Em G7 C
While look - ing for true hap - pi - ness en - twined with - in some star,
And all the time it was down deep with - in the heart of me.
For thoughts that dwell with - in my mind are whol - ly re - ar - ranged.
And in this lov - ing Spir - it my true self I can re - veal.
F F7 Gm G7 C
Or in tran - scend - ent mys - tic rites, or cos - mic mys - ter - ies,
I've found that my own be - ing lives with - in a Spir - it whole,
And so I need no long - er roam to find true hap - pi - ness,
I know that in - ward hap - pi - ness is ev - er there to seek,
F E E7 F A7 D7 G7 C7 F
Or in the deep il - lu - sions born in psy - chic ec - sta - cies.
Its king-dom pow'r and glo - ry fills my ver - y mind and soul.
For I am born to vic - to - ry through my own know-ing - ness.
And joy, and hope, and har - mo - ny are mine if I but speak.

Knowing

(What a Glorious Thought)

Thos. L. McClellan
Anthony J. Showalter, 1887
1. What a glo - rious tho't, what a joy di-vine, Know-ing that my God and I are one; What a bless - ed - ness, what a peace is mine, Know - ing that my God and I are one;
2. What have I to doubt, what have I to fear, Know-ing that my God and I are one; In my mind I know, with con - vic - tion clear, That my God and I are ev - er one.
3. O to feel the joy, that is in my heart, Know-ing that my God and I are one; More a - bun-dant - ly, as new mo-ments start, I shall know my God and I are one.
Refrain
Know - ing, Know - ing, Know-ing my life has just be - gun;
(More of truth know - ing, Joy ev - er grow - ing,)
Know - ing, Know - ing, Ev - er-more my God and I are one.
(His love be-stow-ing, And to me flow - ing,)
G C D7 G C G D7 G

103 There Shall Be Showers of Blessing

Daniel W. Whittle
Adapted by Christina Hovemann
James McGranahan
Arranged by T. L. M.
1. There shall be show-ers of bless-ing, An-sw'ring when-ev-er you call, Spir-it for-ev-er ex-press-ing, Giv-ing it-self un-to all.
2. There shall be show-ers of bless-ing, Bring-ing God's sub-stance a-new, Free-ly re-spond-ing, and press-ing More of God's love in-to view.
3. There shall be show-ers of bless-ing, Quick-ly re-leased at your knock, Head-ing your way, and pro-gress-ing Right thru the door you un-lock.
4. There shall be show-ers of bless-ing, O-pen your heart to re-ceive, Mind-ful that you are pos-sess-ing That which you ful-ly be-lieve.
Chorus
Show-ers of bless-ing, When we learn not to im-pede, O-pen up-on us ex-press-ing God's full a-bun-dance in-deed.

We Praise Thee, O God

Wm. P. Mackay, adapted

John J. Husband

F
C7
F
1. We praise Thee, O God, For the Spir - it of light,
2. All glo - ry and praise For Thy like - ness with - in;
3. Re - joice and be glad; Let the Son in you shine;
Bb
F
C
That has shown us Thy good - ness And scat - tered our night.
As the sons of the Fa - ther, Our tri - umphs be - gin.
Give praise and thanks - giv - ing For love that's Di - vine.
Refrain
F
Bb
F
Bb
F
C
Hal - le - lu - jah! Thine the glo - ry; Hal - le - lu - jah! a - gain!
F
Bb
F
Bb
F
C7
F
Hal - le - lu - jah! Thine the glo - ry; We praise Thee. A - men.

From "Religious Science Hymnal". Used by permission of Dodd, Mead & Co.

105 This Is You

Jill Gerhard | Jill Gerhard

G B7 Em G7
1. How mar - ve - lous, how won - der - ful the Un - i - ver - sal Love As
2. When hap - pen - ings are neg - a - tive, when ev - ery - thing seems wrong, Re -
3. The Peace of God is not far off, it nes - tles in our hearts, So
C D7 G D7
man - i - fest - ed here in you and me I
mem - ber that your at - ti - tude's the key De -
let's dis - cov - er God with - in us all This
G B7 Em G7
look at you and see in you the God - po - ten - tial there; This
lib - erate - ly, then, bring to mind the tho'ts of har - mo - ny; It
is the way to Peace a - mong the na - tions of the earth; Just
C D7 G G7 Chorus
is the real You in Re - a - li - ty
will re - flect in - to your life, you'll see So
know that God is liv - ing in us all

C Cm G D7
let the In - fin - ite Love shine through, This is you,
G G7 C Cm G
real - ly you, Be - lieve God's Life is the heart of you,
A7 D7 G B7
Wait no long - er to know that it's true, How mar-ve-lous, how won-der - ful the
Em G7 C D7 G
Un - i - ver - sal Love, As man - i - fest - ed here in you and me.

106 Are You Ready, Willing and Able

Betty S. Taylor

Betty S. Taylor
Arr. Maurine J. Bailey

D Fdim D
Are you read-y, and will-ing, and a - ble? Do you
G D A7
see the dream that can come true to - day. Are you read-y, and
will-ing, and a - ble? If you are, God will show you the
D Fdim
way. If you're read-y, and will-ing, and a -
D D7 G
ble, you must see your dream com - plet - ed come what may.

D
Are you ready-y, will-ing, and a-ble? If you
A7 D D7 G
are, then get start-ed to-day. Are you read-y,
D B A7
will-ing, and a-ble? If you are, then get start-ed to-
D p A7 D
day. If you are, then get start-ed to-day.
D pp A7 D
If you are, then get start-ed to-day.

107

In the Twinkling of an Eye

Edna Mohr Dooley
A.S.C.A.P.
Edna Mohr Dooley
A.S.C.A.P.
C
G7
1. In the twink-ling of an eye You can change the
2. In a mo-ment God re-plies To the pray'r you
3. In the twink-ling of an eye You can change the
mf
C
Gm
A7
world you live in. Your world re-sponds to
now are us-ing. The mir-a-cles of
world a-round you. Your thoughts be-come the
D7
A7
D7
G7
your com-mand At the mo-ment it is giv-en.
life de-pend On the thoughts of your own choos-ing.
world you seek And the loved ones that sur-round you.

Dedicated to the Rev. Thomas A. Johnson

C G7
In the twink - ling of an eye A new thought can
In a mo - ment God re - sponds To a per - fect
In the twink - ling of an eye You re - spond to
E7 Dm7 Cdim C B7 Gm
change your day. Just make your se - lec - tion And change your di -
faith in pray'r. There's in - stant re - a - tion, Spon - ta - ne - ous
how you pray; For God's love en - folds you, Sus - tains and up -
A7 Dm A7 Dm G7 C
rec - tion; It's all in the way the way you pray.
ac - tion; Be - lieve it, and lo! and lo! it's there.
holds you, Right now on a bright a bright new day.

108 It Is True

Thos. L. McClellan
Thos. L. McClellan
G Gdim G D7 G B7 Emi E7 Emi6 A7
1. There is a na - ture with - in ev - ery one, since time be - gan;
2. There is a pow'r that re - sponds to each need, dis - pers - ing fear;
3. There is a spir - it that seeks to in - spire the will - ing mind;
D7 Ddim D7 G B7 Emi E+ E7 Emi6 Edim7 D7
There is a life that makes each one a son, with - in God's plan;
There is a truth by which men shall be freed, for those who hear;
There is an ef - fort sus - tained by de - sire, by which men find;
G Gdim G D7 G B7 Emi C B
There is a pres - ence that each heart can feel, that keeps one strong;
There is a wis - dom di - rect - ing its beam, as thoughts are sown;
There is a way through Di - vine con-scious-ness, that makes men whole;
C Cdim C Cdim Cmi G Gdim G E+ E7 A9 D7 G
There is a love ev - ery one can re - veal, that brings a song.
There is a faith that ful - fills ev - ery dream, the ra - diance known.
There is a peace that is wait - ing to bless, with - in the soul.

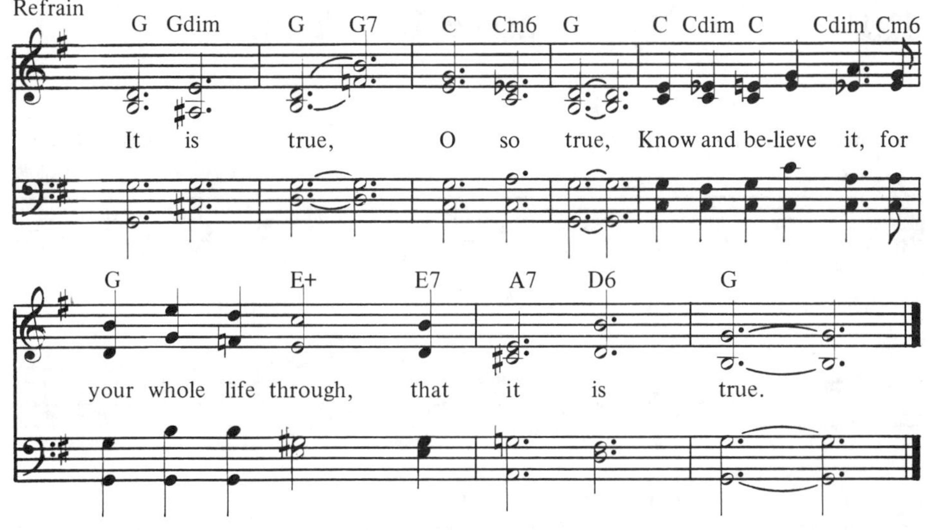

Refrain
G Gdim G G7 C Cm6 G C Cdim C Cdim Cm6
It is true, O so true, Know and be-lieve it, for
G E+ E7 A7 D6 G
your whole life through, that it is true.

You Can Smile

109

Anon., Vs. 1
Thos. L. McClellan, Vs. 2-4

Anon.

C7 F C7 F B♭ C7 F B♭ F C7 F

1. You can smile, when you can't say a word; You can
smile, tho' you can not be heard; You can smile be it
cloud-y or fair; You can smile an-y-time an-y-where.

2. You can sing a new song on life's way; You can
sing a new song as you pray; You can sing a new
song come what may; You can sing a new song ev-ery day.

3. You can know and your faith will show how; You can
know all that God would en-dow; You can know all your
mind will al-low; You can know life a-bun-dant right now.

4. You can be more of what you de-sire; You can
be when you real-ly as-spire; You can be when your
heart is on fire; You can be and ful-fill-ment ac-quire.

110 My Creative Intention

Medium tempo, with feeling
Carmen Moshier
G7 Cmaj7 Am Dm7 Gsus
There's a Cre - a - tive In - ten - tion with - in me,
G7 Dm7 G7 B CM7 Dm
There's a Cre - a - tive Ex - press - ion that will be.
G7 C D♯dim G7 Dm G7 G+ C6
I'll lis - ten, lis - ten with all I can, "Lis - ten, lis - ten" will show the plan,
A A7 Dm G7
God will show me just what I am, there's a pur - pose for me!

a tempo
G7
CM7
Am
Dm7
Gsus
There's a di - vine plan wrapped up in my be - ing,

G7
Dm7
G7
B
CM7
Dm7
G7
There's a di - vine plan a - wait - ing my see - ing.

C
D♯dim
G7
Dm
G7
G+
C
I now let go of all ob-sta-cles; Fear can no long-er block my goals,

molto rit.
Repeat this page
A
A7
Dm7
G7
G+
A♭7
C
I'm a chan-nel ex-press-ing free the di-vine plan com-ing through me.

111 I Am

Thos. L. McClellan | Thos. L. McClellan

F D+ D7 G7 C7 F
1. From now on I'll walk with con-fi-dence, And I'll walk with dig-ni - ty;
2. I shall let di-vine ac - tiv-i-ty Now ex-press in full-er ways;
Bb Bbm F D+ D7 G7 C7
I'll re-spond to Mind be - yond mere sense, And live and move and be.
I shall hear the deep-er har-mo-ny, And live in love and praise.
Refrain
F Bb Bbm F F7 Bb F G7 C7
For I know I am That I am, And my Life is God in me, as me;
F F7 Bb Fdim F rit. Dm6 C7 F
And my heart sings out in ac-cents free: The I Am is the real, real me.

What Greater Pearl

LAQUIPARLE
Thos. L. McClellan
From the Dakota Indian Hymnal
Cm Fm Cm G G7 Cm Bb Bb7
1. What great - er pearl hath man than his mind, Re - ceiv - er
2. What great - er moun - tain shall each man move, Than his own
C G7 Cm Ab Fm6 Cm D7 D+ Gm
of all thought; What great-er pearl hath man than his heart,
faith shall prove; What great-er oaks shall from a - corns grow,
Cm Bb Eb F G7 Cm Fm
In - spir - ing love shown, felt, or sought; What great - er pearl hath
Than Self a - ware - ness man shall know; What great - er won - ders
Cm G G7 Cm Bb Bb7 C G7 Cm
man than his soul, Cre - a - tive Spir - it whole.
shall set man free, Than one's own choice to be.

113 Let's Be!

Words and Music by Carmen
Medium tempo, with feeling
C Cdim Dm Dm7 G7 G9 Ddim C C7
Let's be what we're made to be, Is - n't this our des - ti - ny?
A7 A+ A D7 G7 G+7 C
Let's get start - ed now to - day, Up - ward on our way.
Cdim Dm Dm7 G7 Ddim C C7
Let's be what we real - ly are, Seek and find our in - ner star;
A7 A+ A D7 G7 C
Let's go for - ward in the light, Fac - es shin - ing bright.

2nd time much slower
Am Em Cdim B7 Em
Sons of God, Un - lim - it - ed are we;
2nd time, molto rit.
Am F♯dim G D7 G7
Let us prove The truth that sets us free.
C Cdim Dm Dm7 G7 Ddim C C7
Let's ac - cept our high - est good, Know - ing we're in broth - er - hood,
2nd time, molto rit. to end
Repeat this page
A7 A+ A D7 G7 C
Now the good in all we see, Let's don't wait, LET'S BE!

114 Believe and Know

Marjorie Hughes, Vs. 1
Alvin D. St. John, Vs. 2
Thos. L. McClellan
C G7 Cdim C A7 D7
1. Be - lieve and know you're in His pres - ence;
2. I live and know I'm in His pres - ence;
Gdim G7 Cm6 C
His lov - ing Spir - it now dwells in you.
His lov - ing Spir - it now dwells in me.
Cm6 C Cm G
You know He is the Life you live;
I know He is the Life I live;
D+ G D7 G7 G+7
and ev - 'ry time you give your-self to Him, your cup o'er - flows!
and ev - 'ry time I give my - self to Him, my cup o'er - flows!

C G7 Cdim C A7 D7
You use His mind; His heart you live in,
I use His mind; His heart I live in,
Gdim G7 C
so you're se - cure e - ter - nal - ly!
so I'm se - cure e - ter - nal - ly!
E7 Am F Fm C
His love's so great, you see, He knows you're per - fect!
His love's so great, I see, He knows I'm per - fect!
Cdim C D7 G7 C
So just ac - cept and let it be!
So I ac - cept and let it be!

115

Let Go, Let God

Carmen Moshier

Carmen Moshier

F♯dim7 Fm7 B♭ Fdim E♭
1. Let go of fear, it's noth-ing - ness!
2. Let go re - gret, and yes-ter - year,
F♯dim7 Fm7 B♭ Fdim E♭ Gdim
Take hold of good, it's here to bless.
Let go and see your life is here.
E♭7 A♭ C7 Fm D7 E♭
There's on - ly love for you to share,
There's on - ly God, a whole new view,
F9 molto rit. Fm7 B♭7
The love is yours if you would dare.
Let go to see it come through you.

F♯dim7
Fm7
B♭
Fdim
E♭
a tempo
Let go of doubt, you're not a - lone.
Let go of strain, and toil and care.
F♯dim7
Fm7
B♭
Fdim
E♭
Gdim
Take hold of good, it's yours to own,
Let go and see the whole-ness there,
E♭7
A♭
C7
Fm
D7
E♭
There's on - ly faith to see you through;
There's on - ly God to live AS you,
F9
D♭7
B♭9
E♭6
molto rit.
Let go, let God ex - press through you!
Let go to let God live AS you!

116 Now Power

Thos. L. McClellan
Thos. L. McClellan
F C7 F C7 F F7 B♭
O there is Now Pow - er, yes there is Now Pow - er and the
is Now Pow - er, yes there is Now Pow - er and it's
F B♭ F
1. G7 C
2. G9 C7 F
great sup - ply flows full and free. O there
al - ways there for you and me. Our
B♭ F C7 F B♭ F
yes - ter - days are just mem - o - ries, To - mor - row is still a
C G7 C7 F F7 B♭ Fdim
dream; So right now to - day this ver - y mo - ment

Dedicated to the Rev. Dr. Leo Fishbeck, of Glendale, whose message inspired this song.

G7
C G7 C7
F C7 F C7
let that Pow - er stream. O there is Now Pow-er, yes there
F F7 B♭
F B♭ F
G7 C
is Now Pow-er so en - er - gize and real - ly see. O there
F C7 F C7
F F7 B♭
F C7
is Now Pow-er, yes there is Now Pow-er so real - ly live and
CODA
F
F Fdim C9 C+
F6 F
be. Real - ly feel that Pow - er.

Life Is for Living

Carmen Moshier

Carmen Moshier

Bb
1. Life is for liv - ing,
2. Life is for lov - ing,
A7
Cm7
F7
what - ev - er you will live for, you will give.
what - ev - er you will love e - nough is yours.
Cm7
F7
Cm
Cm7
F7
Life is for giv - ing,
Life is for shar - ing,
A7
Bb
Cm9
F+
what - ev - er you will give to life will live.
what - ev - er you will share with oth - ers grows.
Bb
Life is for do - ing,
Life is for be - ing,

Bb Bb7 Bb+7 Eb
for liv - ing, giv - ing, do - ing, learn - ing how,
for lov - ing, shar - ing, be - ing, learn - ing how,
A+ A7 Bb6 Ddim G7 Cm7
Life is for you, and life is for me, Life is for
Life is for you, and life is for me, Life is for
F7
1st ending
Bb Gm Cm7 Dm F7
Repeat to beginning
liv - ing now!
liv - ing
2nd ending
molto ritard
Bb7 Cm7 F7 Gb
now! Life is for liv - ing now!
Ebm Bb6

Stay Alive!

Thos. L. McClellan

Carmen Moshier

Lively
Eb
Gm
Fm
Bb7
1. Stay a - live for as long as you live,
2. Stay a - wake to the Truth that you learn,
3. Stay a - ware of the Christ with - in you,
Fm
Bb7
Eb
And per - ceive all that life has to give;
And the spir - it of joy shall re - turn;
And you'll find that your life will re - new;
Eb7
Ab
Abm6
With true dig - ni - ty O man, find the glo - ry of God's plan,
There's no need to ev - er fret, just re - vise the path you've set,
Free each nerve and ev - 'ry cell, lift your thots 'til all is well,
Eb
Bb7
Eb
Eb7
Stay a - live for as long as you live!

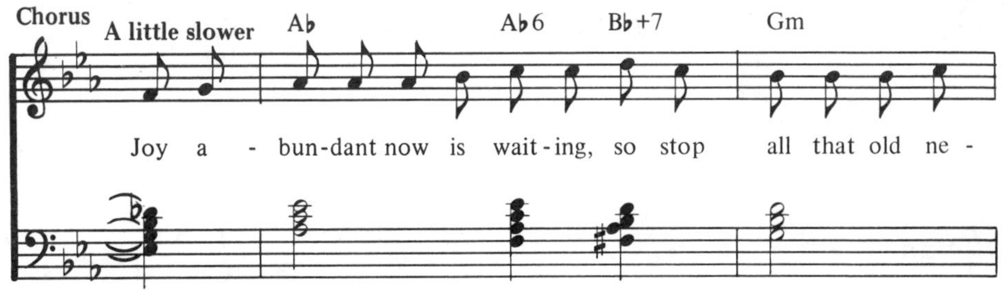
Chorus
A little slower
Ab
Ab6
Bb+7
Gm
Joy a - bun-dant now is wait - ing, so stop all that old ne -

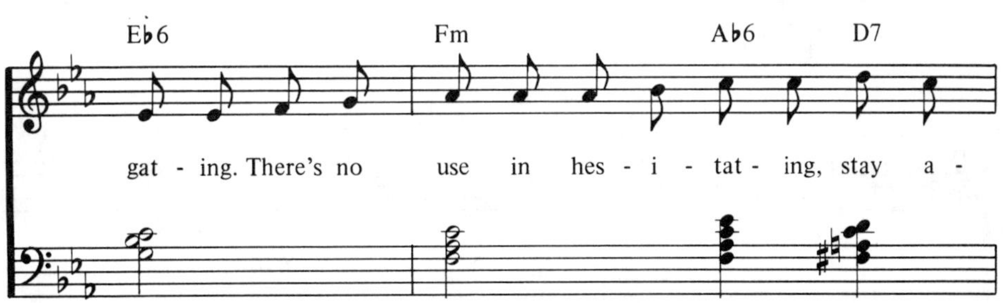
Eb6
Fm
Ab6
D7
gat - ing. There's no use in hes - i - tat - ing, stay a -

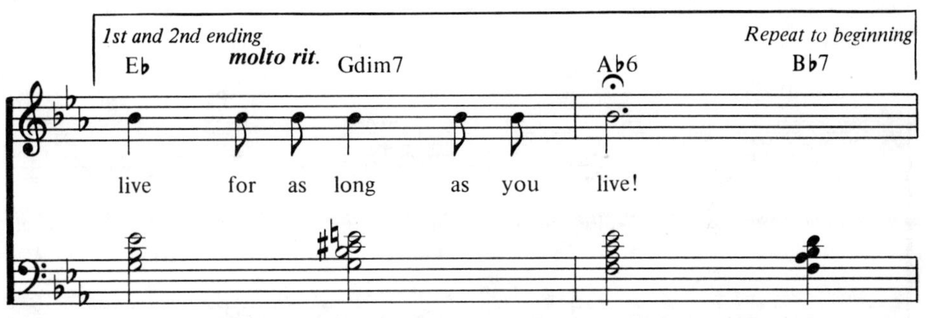
1st and 2nd ending
Repeat to beginning
Eb
molto rit.
Gdim7
Ab6
Bb7
live for as long as you live!

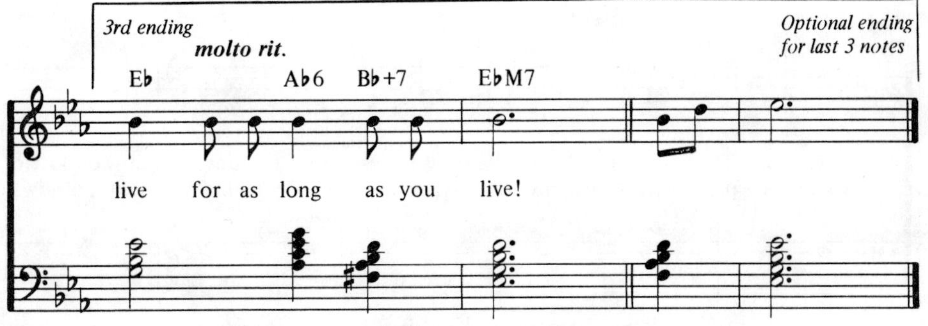
3rd ending
molto rit.
Optional ending
for last 3 notes
Eb
Ab6
Bb+7
EbM7
live for as long as you live!

119 In My Heart There's a Song

Thos. L. McClellan
Thos. L. McClellan
F F7 B♭6 G G7 C7
1. In my heart there's a song, that I sing the day long, of the love that my
2. O my song is for aye, it's my song as I pray, for my heart feels the
F F7 B♭6
God gives to me; And my joy shall a - bound in this kin - ship I've
in - fi - nite gleam; Yes, my heart is a - glow, for with - in I now
G G7 C7 F B♭ Gdim D♭7
found, of my in - fi - nite re - al - i - ty. O the joy I have shall
know that my God is for - ev - er su - preme. O I sing the truth I
F B♭+ D7 G7 Dm6 C7 F
e'er con - fess to my own grate - ful - ness; For I know on Life's
would ex - press with - in my be - ing - ness; In my soul I now

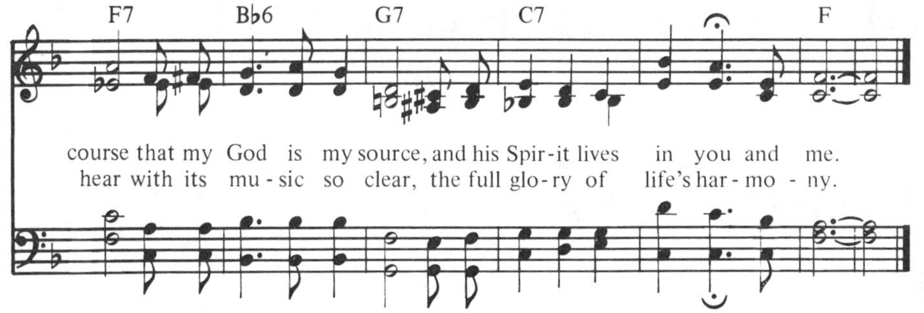
F7 B♭6 G7 C7 F
course that my God is my source, and his Spir-it lives in you and me.
hear with its mu-sic so clear, the full glo-ry of life's har-mo-ny.

God Is My Perfect Life 120

Anonymous

Viennese Melody

F Fdim F B♭ F G7

1. God is my per - fect life: Thro' Him I live. God is my
2. God is my per - fect guide: Thro' Him I'm led. God is my
3. God is my per - fect peace: Thro' Him I rest. God is my

C7 F Fdim F B♭ F

per - fect gift: Thro' Him I give. God is my per - fect light:
per - fect word: Thro' Him I'm fed. God is my per - fect good:
per - fect joy: Thro' Him I'm blest. God is my per - fect will:

G7 C7 F

Thro' Him I see. God is my per-fect voice: He speaks thro' me.
My way is clear. God is my per-fect love, And He is here.
Thro' me 'tis done. God is my per-fect all, And We are one.

From "Unity Song Selections"

121 I Can Sing about the Glories

Christina Hovemann
Christina Hovemann
Eb Bbm6 C Fm
1. I can sing a-bout the glo-ries in the king-dom of our God;
2. I can praise the man-y won-ders man-i-fest in realms a-bove;
3. I can stud-y more a-bout the one-ness of the u-ni-verse;
Fm7 Bb Eb
I can talk a-bout the beau-ties of the world in which we trod;
I can mar-vel at the mir-a-cles ac-com-plished by His love;
I can try to un-der-stand its scope and func-tions so di-verse;
Bbm6 C7 Fm C7 Fm
But, to bring the won-drous king-dom in-to full re-al-i-ty,
But, to re-a-lize the full-ness of its ac-tion, I must see:
But, to ful-ly com-pre-hend the on-ly Pow-er, I must see:
Adim Eb Fm7 Bb6 Bb7 Eb Bb
Per-fect truth must dwell in me; In me,
Per-fect love in-dwell-ing me; In me,
Per-fect Spir-it dwells in me; In me,
(in me)
(in me)

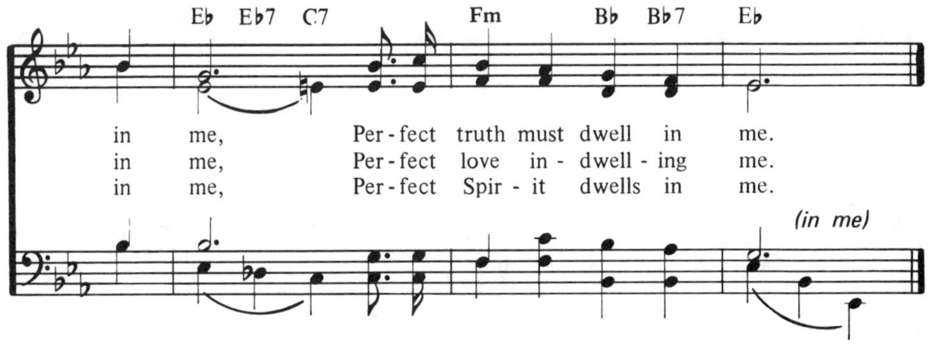
Eb Eb7 C7 Fm Bb Bb7 Eb
in me, Per-fect truth must dwell in me.
in me, Per-fect love in-dwell-ing me.
in me, Per-fect Spir-it dwells in me.
(in me)

Give a Little More 122

Nadene McClellan | Nadene McClellan

G Gdim G
Give, give, give, give, give a lit-tle more, And watch sup-ply keep grow-ing;

Gdim Am D7
Live, live, live, live, live a lit-tle more, There's so much in the know-ing.

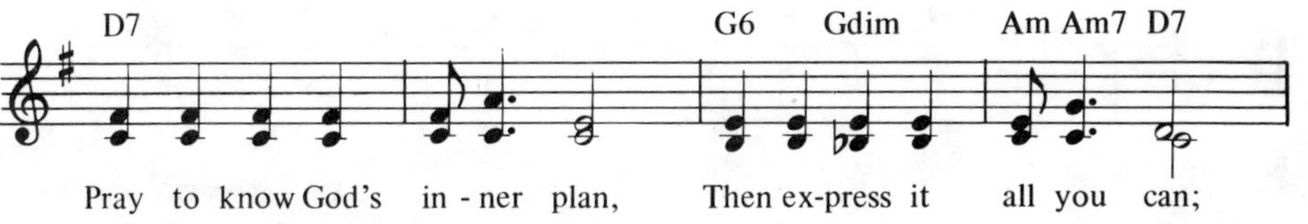
D7 G6 Gdim Am Am7 D7
Pray to know God's in-ner plan, Then ex-press it all you can;

G A7 D7 G
Love, love, love, love, love a lit-tle more, God's bless-ing is o'er-flow-ing.

123 Why

NETTLETON
American Folk Tune
John Wyeth's coll., 1813
Thos. L. McClellan
1. Why be filled with all thy wor - ry, Why be filled with all thy doubt,
2. Why be filled with in - de - ci - sion, Why be tied up in a knot,
3. May good cheer now fill thy be - ing, And the joy of life be thine,
Why should we go hur - ry - scur - ry, And in cir - cles race a - bout?
Why not seek the in - ner vi - sion, That's re - vealed in qui - et thought?
May di - rec - tion of our see - ing, Find the pow'r of God di - vine;
God with - in shall ev - er guide us, And for - ev - er holds the key;
As His truth and love de - cide us, Mak - ing pur - pose clear and strong,
With as - sur - ance now be - hold it, As our voice in song we raise,
Why should we let dark - ness hide us, When the light will set us free.
Var - ied ways shall not di - vide us, And our heart will sing a song.
And per - ceiv - ing now en - fold it, And be filled with love and praise.

Sing a Song

Thos. L. McClellan

Thos. L. McClellan

F
C7
1. Sing a song of cheer and hap - pi - ness, Sing a song in your heart to - day;
2. Sing a song of cheer right where you are, Sing a song for your whole life through;
3. Sing a song with sun-shine in your smile, See the rain - bows of joy ap - pear;
Cdim C7
C+ F
Let the mu - sic in you ra - di - ate, Let those joy - ful tones hold sway.
Har - mo - nize with vi - brant life that lives Deep with - in the heart of you.
Sing a song and know the liv - ing God Ev - er is and now is near.
F7
B♭
Sing a song a - long life's rhyth - mic way, Sing and keep all those blues a - way;
Feel the Spir - it urg - ing to re - new, Sing and know that it's real - ly true;
Live and be, and sing so all can hear Love's true mel - o - dies of good cheer;
F
B♭
Fdim
F
C7
F
Let your heart sing "Al - le - lu - ia", Sing a joy - ful song to - day.

125 Have a Happy Heart

Thos. L. McClellan
Thos. L. McClellan
C F C F C G7 Cdim
1. Sing and have a hap - py heart, Be - gin to - day; (O you can)
2. You can start right where you are, And here's a clue; (Just know that)
C F C D7 G7
Sing and have a hap - py heart, All a - long life's way;
You can start right where you are, Let your smile shine through;
C F C F C
Sing and have a hap - py heart, Toss your cares a - way; Be
You can start right where you are, In the heart of you; Be
F C D7 G7
of good cheer, and nev - er fear, for God is near; So
C F C F C
have a hap - py heart Live a hap - py heart,
G7 C
Be a hap - py heart to - day. (Right now to - day.)

God's Melody of Life

Georgiana Tree West | Georgiana Tree West

Eb Bb7 Eb Bb7 Eb Ab Eb
I am God's mel - o - dy of life, He sings His song through me.
Bb7 Eb Bb7 Eb Ab Bb7 Eb
I am God's rhy-thm and har - mo - ny, He sings His song through me.
Cmi Eb Cmi Eb Cmi Bb7
A song of life, Of ra - diant life, Of life so full and free.
Eb Bb7 Eb Bb7 Eb Ab Bb7 Eb
I am God's mel - o - dy of life, He sings His song through me.

Note: For an optional ending repeat last phrase two additional times.

127 Over the Mountain

Alvin D. St. John
Meredith Willson
1. God is the Life that lives through me,
Liv - ing a life that I can be!
I know the Life that lives through me
Lives through the world I love.
Refrain
O - ver the moun - tain, o - ver the sea,
God is the Life that lives in me
I feel the Life that I can be
Fill - ing the world I love.

2. God is the Light that shines through me,
Showing the way that I can be!
I know the Light that shines through me
Shines in the world I love.

Over the mountain, over the sea,
God is the Light that shines in me,
Showing the way that I can be,
Lighting the way of Love. (S.M. p. 538)

3. God is the Truth that speaks through me,
Telling me what I ought to be;
I know the Truth that speaks through me
Calls to the world I love.

Over the mountain, over the sea,
I hear the Truth that speaks to me:
"God is the way that I can be!
God is the way to love." (S.M. p. 541)

4. God is the Joy that sings through me,
Lifting the load so I can be
Filled with the Joy of Christ in me,
Knowing the pow'r of Love.

Over the mountain, over the sea,
God is the Joy that sings through me,
Lifting the load so I can be
Filled with the pow'r of Love. (S.M. p. 538)

5. I am the Life of God in me,
I am the Light, eternally!
I am the Truth forever free,
I am the Joy of Love.

Over the mountain, over the sea,
I know the Light of Life in me;
I know the Truth that sets me free,
God is the Joy I love!

128 Within My Heart

Alvin D. St. John

Thos. L. McClellan

1. I have the light of Life with-in me, Al-to-geth-er clear and bright!
2. I have the love of God with-in me, Man-i-fest-ing ev-er new;
3. I have the song of God with-in me, Har-mo-niz-ing through and through;
It is the Life of God re-new-ing me, Mak-ing ev-ery-thing all right!
It is the Light of Life ex-press-ing me, And in ev-ery-thing I do.
It is the Song of Heav-en heal-ing me, Mak-ing all good things come true.
Refrain
With-in my heart I hear a glo-rious mel-o-dy, It sings a
song to me of joy and har-mo-ny; With-in my heart the rhy-thm
of this mel-o-dy Is sing-ing on and on to me.

Down Deep in Your Heart

Thos. L. McClellan
Thos. L. McClellan
C7 F C7 F
1. If you real - ly love and sing down deep in your heart, You will
2. If you have a lov - ing thought down deep in your heart, It will
3. If you want a - bun-dant life down deep in your heart, You will
G7 C G7 C7 F C7 F
have true joy and zest; If you real - ly love and sing down
flow right back to you; If you have a lov - ing thought down
find it as you pray; If you want a - bun - dant life down
G9 C7 F
deep in your heart, Your life tru - ly will be blessed.
deep in your heart, You will feel the ra - di - ance too.
deep in your heart, You can have it now to - day.
CODA (After last verse)
F rit. 1. G9 C7 F 2. G9 C7 C+ F
Way down deep, way down deep in your heart! deep in your heart!

130 I Would Ever Walk with Thee

Thos. L. McClellan
AMERICAN SPIRITUAL
Arr. by Thos. L. McClellan
Bb F7 Bbdim7 Bb
1. If I fal - ter in life's throng, Guide me Fa - ther from all wrong;
2. If with fear my mind runs cold, By Thy strength my tho'ts re - mold;
3. Tho' with - in I feel de - spair, Still I'll find Thy love is there;
Bb7 Eb Bb Gb7 F7 Bb
And I'll praise Thee with a song In my heart, as I walk close with Thee.
And re - newed they shall un - fold In my mind, as I walk close with Thee.
When I seek re - deem-ing care In my soul, as I walk close with Thee.
Refrain
F7 Bbdim7 Bb
I would ev - er walk with Thee, In my be-ing won - drous-ly;
Bb7 Eb Bb Gb7 F7 Bb
Lord, di-rect my des - ti - ny, As I walk, dear Lord, close with Thee.

God's Love Is Deep within Me 131

SWING LOW
Anon. version
American Spiritual
God's Love / God's Peace / God's Joy is deep with-in me, Ev - er sat - is - fy - in' my soul, God's Love / God's Peace / God's Joy is
deep with - in me, Ev-er sat - is - fy - in' my soul.
Fine
1. I looked deep with- in me and what did I see? Ev - er sat - is - fy - in' my soul, The Love of God so full and free Ev - er sat - is - fy - in' my soul.
2. When I feel the peace that sets me free, Ev - er sat - is - fy - in' my soul, I know that I am one with Thee, Ev - er sat - is - fy - in' my soul.
Last time D. C. al Fine

132 In-a My Heart

Early American Spiritual
Recast by Thos. L. McClellan
Early American Spiritual
Adapted
D A7 D6 G D G
1. Lord, I want to be more lov - ing In - a my heart, in - a my
2. Yes, I'm goin' to be more cheer-ful In - a my heart, in - a my
3. I shall ra - di-ate God's heav - en In - a my heart, in - a my
D A7 D6 G D
heart, Lord, I want to be more lov - ing in - a my heart.
heart, Yes, I'm goin' to be more cheer-ful in - a my heart.
heart, I shall ra - di-ate God's heav - en in - a my heart.
Refrain
G D
In - a my heart, in - a my heart,
In - a my heart, in - a my heart,
rit. D7 G G7 D
Lord, I want to be more lov - ing in - a my heart.
Yes, I'm goin' to be more cheer-ful in - a my heart.
I shall ra - di-ate God's heav - en in - a my heart.

May Our Hearts Be Always Open 133

Thos. L. McClellan

Thos. L. McClellan

F C7 Gm Gdim C7 C+ F
1. May our hearts be al-ways o-pen, To let Love flow through,
2. May our hearts be calm and stead-y, Tho' dark clouds drift by,
C7 G7 C7
Love that lives in full di-men-sion, Love un-feigned and true;
May Love's sun-shine ev-er glow-ing, Re-move ev-'ry sigh;
F D7 Gm C7 Gm Gdim C7 B♭7 A
May we ev-er be re-cep-tive To God's giv-ing-ness,
Why should we feel lost or lone-ly, Why should we be blue,
B♭ B♭m F D7 Gm C6 F
And, re-spond-ing, e'er ex-press it In our liv-ing-ness.
For we know that God first loved us And cre-a-tion through.

From This Moment On

(A Wedding Prayer)

Thos. L. McClellan Thos. L. McClellan

From this mo - ment on, may two hearts beat as
one, With love and good cheer in a un - ion begun. With pa - tience and trust may their life
be ex - pressed, With joy and ful - fill - ment may their
dreams e'er be blessed. May love - light e - ter -

nal re - main in their thought, Sus - tain - ing for -
ev - er what God now has wrought. O Love
Di - vine, may thy ra - diance reign;
In thy per - fec - tion their vows now or - dain.
CODA
From this mo - ment on. From this mo - ment on.

135 New Age Vision

Vs. 1 & 2 Henry V. Morgan
Vs. 3 Thos. L. McClellan
Based on poem by Julia W. Howe

BATTLE HYMN OF THE REPUBLIC
William Steffe, 1852

1. Mine eyes have seen the com - ing of an age that is to be,
2. My soul has seen the com - ing of a race from sor - row free,
3. My soul has seen the glo - ry of a great re - al - i - ty,
When from ev - ery lim - i - ta - tion shall the son of man be free;
In an age of faith and jus - tice, truth and love and lib - er - ty;
For it sees the ev - er pres- ent Christ with - in both you and me;
For the age is rich in prom - ise and my soul has eyes to see —
And I sing of love's great tri - umph in that year of jub - i - lee —
And I know that God's great king - dom is, and shall for - ev - er be —
God's truth is march-ing on.
God's truth is march-ing on.
God's truth is march-ing on.
REFRAIN
Glo - ry, glo - ry, hal - le -

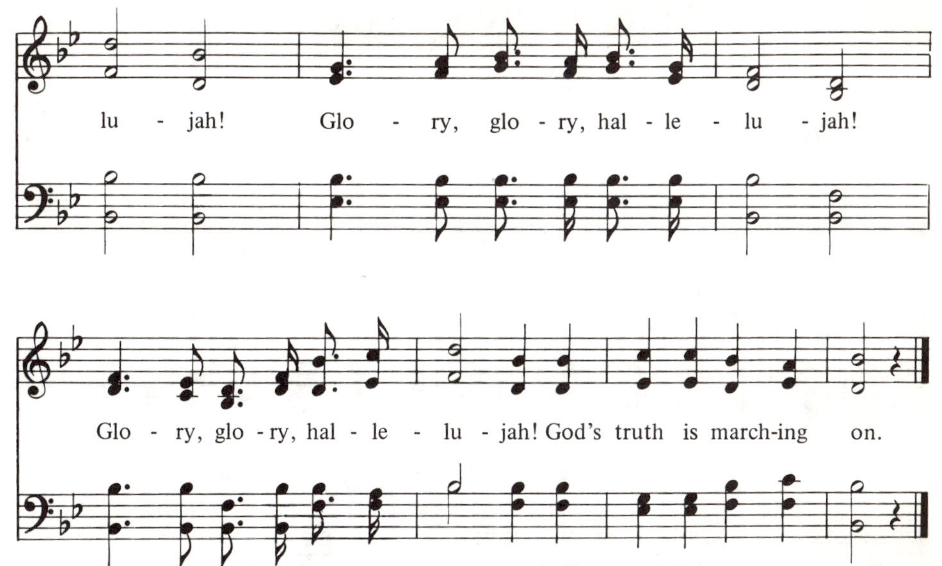

lu - jah! Glo - ry, glo - ry, hal - le - lu - jah!
Glo - ry, glo - ry, hal - le - lu - jah! God's truth is march-ing on.

Ring Out the Old, Ring In the New 136

Alfred Tennyson, 1850, alt.

WALTHAM
J. Baptiste Calkin, 1872

1. Ring out the old, ring in the new, Ring hap- py bells, a - cross the snow;
2. Ring out the man-ners cold and rude, The fi -ery slan-der and the spite;
3. Ring in the val- iant man and free, The lar -ger heart, the kind-lier hand;

The year is go - ing, let him go; Ring out the false, ring in the true.
Ring in the love of truth and right, Ring in the high de - sire of good.
Ring out the dark-ness of the land, Ring in the light that is to be.

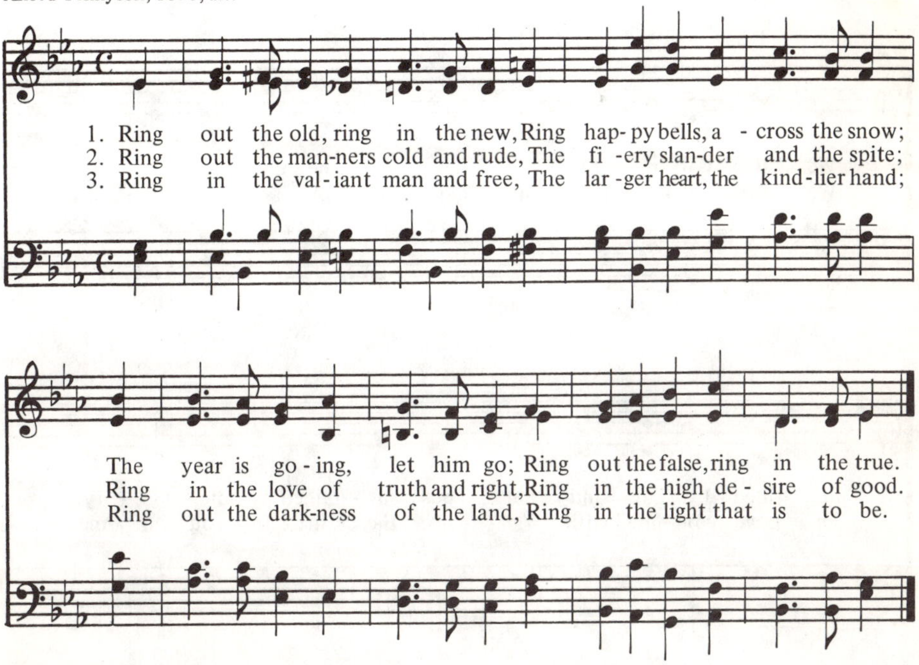

137

The Hope of Nations

Thos. L. McClellan
George J. Webb, 1837
G C G D7
1. We sing the hope of na - tions, God's Light in ev - 'ry soul,
2. We sing of Mind in ac - tion, in - spir - ing high - er thought,
G C G D7 G
The king - dom, pow'r and glo - ry that is cre - a - tion's goal.
Con - trol - ling our e - mo - tions, or - dain - ing what is sought.
D7 G C G C G D7
We sing of in - nate Whole - ness, of one's own choice to be,
We sing of Life a - bun - dant from moun - tains to the sea,
G C G D7 G
Ful - filled by Law and Pur - pose, sus - tained by dig - ni - ty.
Of Love com - bined with Wis - dom, the Christ in you and me.

O Day of Light and Gladness

LANCASHIRE

Frederick L. Hosmer, 1903 Henry T. Smart, 1836

1. O day of light and glad - ness, Of proph - e - cy and song,
2. Earth feels the sea-son's joy - ance; From moun-tain range to sea
3. O Lord of life e - ter - nal, To thee our hearts up - raise
What thoughts with-in us wak - en, What hal-lowed mem-'ries throng!
The tides of life are flow - ing, Fresh, man - i - fold and free.
The East-er song of glad - ness, The Pass-o - ver of praise.
The soul's hor - i - zon wid - ens, Past, pres-ent, fu - ture blend;
In val - ley and on up - land, By for-est path - ways dim,
Thine are the man - y man - sions, The dead die not to thee,
And ris - es on our vi - sion The life that hath no end.
All na - ture lifts in cho - rus The res - sur - ec - tion hymn.
They dwell with - in thy full - ness For all e - ter - ni - ty.

139 Spring Has Now Unwrapped the Flowers

The Oxford Book of Carols, 1928
Trans. by Percy Dearmer

TEMPUS ADEST FLORIDUM
Theodoric Petri's Piae Cantiones, 1582
Harmonized by Martin Shaw, 1928

1. Spring has now un - wrapped the flowers, Day is fast re - viv - ing,
2. Through each won - der of fair days God him-self ex - press - es;
3. Praise the Mak - er, all ye saints; He with glo - ry girt you,

Life in all her grow-ing powers Toward the light is striv - ing;
Beau-ty fol-lows all his ways, As the world he bless - es;
He who skies and mead-ows paints Fash - ioned all your vir - tue.

All the world with beau - ty fills, Gold the green en - hanc - ing;
So, as he re - news the earth, Art - ist with - out ri - val,
Praise him, se - ers, he - roes, kings, Her - alds of per - fec - tion;

Flowers make glee a - mong the hills, And set mead-ows danc - ing.
In his grace of glad new birth We must seek re - vi - val.
Broth - ers, praise him, for he brings All to res - ur - rec - tion!

Christ, the Lord Is Risen Today 140

Charles Wesley and others, adapted

EASTER HYMN
from Lyra Davidica, 1708

1. Christ, the Lord is ris'n to - day,
2. Now a - new the Spir - it flows,
3. New a - ware - ness now doth reign,
4. End - less glo - ry to all men,
Al - - le - lu - ia!
Sons of men and an - gels say,
Spring-ing life from death is born,
Let thy thoughts in Truth a - rise,
Can such match - less splen - dor dim,
Al - - le - lu - ia!
Raise your joys and tri - umphs high,
All of na - ture is a - glow,
Sing, O heart and live a - gain,
Sing with joy thy great a - men,
Al - - le - lu - ia!
Sing, ye heav'ns and earth re - ply,
'Tis the res - ur - rec-tion morn,
Let thy ra - diance fill the skies,
Sing thy great tri - um-phal hymn,
Al - - le - lu - ia!

141 Now Thank We All Our God

Abridged from Martin Rinkart
Trans. by Catherine Winkworth
Vs. 2 Thos. L. McClellan

NUN DANKET
Johann Crüger, 1646
Harm. by Felix Mendelssohn

1. Now thank we all our God With heart and hands and voic - es,
2. All praise and thanks to God, The source of all cre - a - tion,
Who won-drous things hath done, In whom his world re - joic - es;
With Un - i - ver - sal Love Dis - played to ev - ery na - tion;
Who, from our moth-ers' arms, Hath blessed us on our way
The one e - ter - nal God, To know and to a - dore;
With count-less gifts of love, And still is ours to - day.
For thus it was, is now, And shall be ev - er - more. A-men.

We Thank Thee, Lord, for This Fair Earth 142

George E. L. Cotton, 1856, adapted

HURSLEY
Adapt. from Katholisches Gesangbuch
Vienna, 1774

F C7 F
1. We thank Thee, Lord, for this fair earth,
2. And though we see such gran - deur fair,
3. So as we gaze with thought - ful eyes,
C7 F C
The ra - diant sky, the flow - ing streams,
More glo - rious still be - comes our sight,
On all that love and law still molds,
Gm D7 Gm C F B♭ C
For all their beau - ty, all their worth,
When we can see in deed and prayer,
A new a - ware - ness now re - plies,
B♭ Csus Dm B♭ F C7 F B♭ F
Thy pow'r and glo - ry on us beams.
A heart that owns thy Spir - it's might.
And in full splen - dor life un - folds. A - men.

143 Come, Ye Thankful People, Come

Henry Alford
Anna L. Barbauld, and others

ST. GEORGE'S WINDSOR
George J. Elvey

1. Come, ye thank-ful peo-ple, come, Raise the song of har-vest home:
2. All the bless-ings of the field, All the stores the gar-dens yield,
3. These to thee, our God, we owe, Source from whom all bless-ings flow;
All is ful-ly gath-ered in, Safe as win-ter storms be-gin;
All the fruit in full sup-ply, Rip-ened un-der sum-mer sky,
And for these our songs we raise Songs of joy and grate-ful praise.
God, our Mak-er, does pro-vide For our wants to be sup-plied;
All that spring with boun-teous hand Scat-ters on re-cep-tive land,
Come, then, thank-ful peo-ple, come, Raise the song of har-vest home;
Come to God's own tem-ple, come, Raise the song of har-vest home.
All that lib-'ral au-tumn pours From her rich-ly flow-ing stores.
Come to God's own tem-ple, come, Raise the song of har-vest home. A-men.

We Come with Rejoicing

KREMSER
Netherlands Folk Tune, 1625
Arr. by Edward Kremser

Christina Hovemann, alt.

1. We come with re - joic - ing, our grat - i - tude voic - ing, That
2. We ev - er shall praise Thee for boun - ty be - stow - ing, For
3. O Lord, we would ev - er with wis - dom dis - cern - ing, Be -

God in his good - ness hath pros - pered our days; With
glo - ri - ous ver - dure from moun - tain to shore; For
hold not a - lone thine a - bun - dance so free; But

joy - ful thanks - giv - ing for more a - bun - dant liv - ing, To
crops that are grow - ing, for barns filled ov - er - flow - ing, We'll
filled with a yearn - ing for truth may we be learn - ing The

geth - er now we sing our glad an - thems of praise.
sing our prais - es, Lord, from our heart ev - er - more.
glo - ry of thy Spir - it for - ev - er to see.

145 Hark! the Herald Angels Sing

MENDELSSOHN
Felix Mendelssohn
Arr. William H. Cummings
Charles Wesley, adapted
1. Hark! the her - ald an - gels sing, "Glo - ry to the new-born King;
2. Christ, by high - est heaven a - dored; Christ, the ev - er - last - ing Lord!
3. Christ - mas bells in full - ness toll, Joy and hope fills heart and soul;
Peace on earth, and mer-cy mild, God and sin - ners rec - on - ciled!"
Tid - ings ech - o from each hill, "Peace on earth, to all good will!"
And the mes - sage deep and clear, Rings through-out the at - mos-phere:
Joy - ful all ye na-tions rise, Join the tri - umph of the skies;
Hail the Prince of love and peace, Hail the Sun of right-eous-ness;
Christ in man shall ev - er bless, Prince of peace in con-scious-ness,
With the an-gel - ic host pro-claim, "Christ is born in Beth-le - hem!"
Christ in man is born and brings, Heal - ing light up - on his wings;
Liv - ing in all men on earth, Christ with - in gives sec - ond birth;

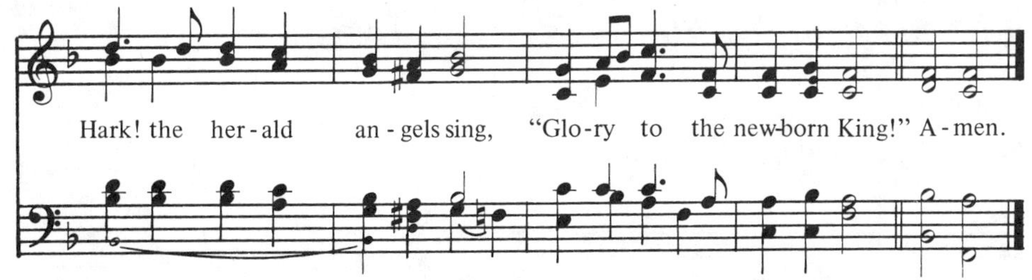
Hark! the her-ald an-gels sing, "Glo-ry to the new-born King!" A-men.

Silent Night, Holy Night 146

Based on Joseph Mohr
Version by Thos. L. McClellan

STILLE NACHT
Franz Gruber

1. Si - lent night, ho - ly night, All is calm, all is bright;
'Round yon man - ger, moth-er and child, Ho - ly in-fant so ten-der and mild,
Sleep in heav-en-ly peace, Sleep in heav - en - ly peace.

2. Si - lent night, ho - ly night, Guid - ing star gives great light;
From a - far the wise men bring Pre-cious gifts to Christ the King,
Prince of love and peace, Prince of love and peace.

3. Si - lent night, ho - ly night, Shep - herds wake with new sight;
An - gel voic - es sing as one, "Un - to you the liv - ing Son,
Christ, the Sav-ior, is born, Christ, the Sav - ior is born."

147 Angels We Have Heard on High

Vs. 1 & 2 Trad. French Carol
Vs. 3 Thos. L. McClellan

GLORIA
Trad. French Carol

1. An-gels we have heard on high, Sweet-ly sing-ing o'er the plains,
2. Shep-herds, why this ju-bi-lee? Why your joy-ous strains pro-long?
3. To the Christ of God we sing, And to truth so long con-cealed,
And the moun-tains in re-ply, Ech-o-ing their joy-ous strains.
What the glad-some ti-dings be Which in-spire your heav'n-ly song?
For in man a new born King, Has this day now been re-vealed.
Refrain
Glo - - - - - - ri-a
in ex-cel-sis De-o.
1.
2.
De - o.

Verse 3 from "Sing With Me" © 1972. Used by permission.

Joy to the World 148

ANTIOCH
Lowell Mason, 1836
from Handel's Messiah, 1742
From Isaac Watts, 1719
1. Joy to the world! the Lord is come: Let earth re - ceive her king; Let ev - ery heart pre - pare him room, And heaven and na - ture sing, And heaven and na - ture sing, And heaven, and heaven and na - ture sing.
2. Joy to the earth! the Sav - ior reigns: Let men their songs em - ploy, While fields and floods, rocks, hills, and plains Re - peat the sound - ing joy, Re - peat the sound - ing joy, Re - peat, re - peat the sound - ing joy.
3. He fills the world with truth and grace, Let all the na - tions prove The glo - ries of his right-eous - ness And won - ders of his love, And won - ders of his love, And won - ders, won - ders of his love.
And heaven and na - ture sing, And heaven and na-ture sing,

149 O Little Town of Bethlehem

Vs. 1 Phillips Brooks, 1868
Vs. 2 & 3 Thos. L. McClellan, 1972

ST. LOUIS
Lewis H. Redner, 1868

1. O lit - tle town of Beth - le - hem, How still we see thee lie!
A - bove thy deep and dream-less sleep The si - lent stars go by!
Yet in thy dark streets shin - eth The ev - er - last - ing light,
The hopes and fears of all the years Are met in thee to - night.
2. We see the light ex - pand - ing, As night turns in - to morn,
And there to bless in con-scious-ness, The Christ of God is born;
How si - lent - ly with - in man The won-drous gift is given
As God im - parts to hu - man hearts The bless-ings of His heaven.
3. O ye who deep - ly slum - ber, A - wak - en and re - joice!
Your an-thems sing and prais - es bring In one har - mon-ious voice;
Like un - to mu - sic swell - ing In full and vi - brant tone,
The Christ with - in that e'er has been, To all men shall be known.

There's a Song in the Air

Josiah G. Holland, 1872, adapted

CHRISTMAS SONG
Karl P. Harrington, 1904

1. There's a song in the air, There's a star in the sky,
There's a mother's deep prayer, In a soft lullaby;
There's a sweet harmony between mother and child,
In an accent of loveliness tender and mild.

2. Let each heart feel the love, And all nations unite,
'Round the one that was born, Filled with radiance and light;
For in stature he grew and awareness of mind,
And the "Father within" was his gift to mankind.

3. Let a tumult of joy In the world now resound,
For this glorious birth Of a truth so profound;
Let us echo our praise and one Spirit enfold,
Which indwelleth all men and the manger of old. Amen.

151 America the Beautiful

Katharine Lee Bates, 1893, 1904

MATERNA
Samuel Augustus Ward, 1882

1. O beautiful for spacious skies, For amber waves of grain,
For purple mountain majesties Above the fruited plain!
America! America! God shed his grace on thee,
And crown thy good with brotherhood From sea to shining sea.

2. O beautiful for pilgrim feet, Whose stern, impassioned stress
A thoroughfare for freedom beat Across the wilderness!
America! America! God mend thine every flaw,
Confirm thy soul in self-control, Thy liberty in law.

3. O beautiful for heroes proved In liberating strife,
Who more than self their country loved, And mercy more than life!
America! America! May God thy gold refine,
Till all success be nobleness, And every gain divine.

4. O beautiful for patriot dream That sees beyond the years
Thine alabaster cities gleam Undimmed by human tears!
America! America! God shed his grace on thee,
And crown thy good with brotherhood From sea to shining sea.

My Country, 'Tis of Thee

AMERICA
Samuel F. Smith
Anon. in "Thesaurus Musicus", 1744
1. My coun - try, 'tis of thee, Sweet land of lib - er - ty,
2. My na - tive coun - try, thee, Land of the no - ble, free;
3. Let mu - sic swell the breeze, And ring from all the trees
4. Our fa - thers' God, to thee, Au - thor of lib - er - ty,
Of thee I sing; Land where my fa - thers died,
Thy name I love; I love thy rocks and rills,
Sweet free - dom's song; Let mor - tal tongues a - wake;
To thee we sing; Long may our land be bright
Land of the pil - grims' pride, From ev - ery
Thy woods and tem - pled hills; My heart with
Let all that breathe par - take; Let rocks their
With free - dom's ho - ly light; Pro - tect us
moun - tain - side Let free - dom ring!
rap - ture thrills, Like that a - bove.
si - lence break, The sound pro - long.
by thy might, Great God, our King. A - men.

153 The Star-Spangled Banner

Francis Scott Key, 1814

John Stafford Smith, 1775

1. O say, can you see, by the dawn's early light,
What so proudly we hailed at the twilight's last gleaming?
Whose broad stripes and bright stars, thro' the perilous fight,
O'er the ramparts we watched, were so gallantly streaming?
2. On the shore, dimly seen thro' the mists of the deep,
Where the foe's haughty host in dread silence reposes,
What is that which the breeze, o'er the towering steep,
As it fitfully blows, half conceals, half discloses?
3. O thus be it ever when freemen shall stand
Between their loved homes and the war's desolation!
Blest with vict'ry and peace, may the heav'n-rescued land
Praise the Pow'r that hath made and preserved us a nation!

And the rock-et's red glare, the bombs burst-ing in air,
Now it catch-es the gleam of the morn-ing's first beam,
Then con-quer we must, when our cause it is just,
Gave proof thro' the night that our flag was still there.
In full glo-ry re-flect-ed now shines on the stream:
And this be our mot-to: "In God is our trust!"
O say, does that Star-span-gled Ban-ner still wave
'Tis the Star-span-gled Ban-ner, O long may it wave
And the Star-span-gled Ban-ner in tri-umph shall wave
O'er the land of the free, and the home of the brave?
O'er the land of the free, and the home of the brave.
O'er the land of the free, and the home of the brave.

154 Ours, O Lord, a Mighty Nation

Fenwick L. Holmes
AUSTRIA
Franz Joseph Haydn, 1797
1. Ours, O Lord, a might-y na-tion, Spread-ing wide from sea to sea;
2. Man is free, and man is mas-ter Of him-self, is king or slave;
3. Lo, at last, the rev-e-la-tion, Comes ful-fill-ment of the dream;
4. Ours, O Lord, a might-y na-tion, Fruit-ful lands from sea to sea;
Ours, the cap-stone of cre-a-tion, Land of hope and lib-er-ty.
Stored in pre-cious al-a-bas-ter, Life is his to spend or save.
God has built Him-self a na-tion, Where the law shall be su-preme.
From the school-house and the stee-ple Peal the bells of lib-er-ty.
In our veins the blood of peo-ple Out of ev-ery land and birth;
His it is to voice his feel-ing, His to wor-ship or re-frain.
For this law let all the liv-ing Joy-ful-ly their voic-es raise
Thanks for men who on the al-tar Layed their lives at free-dom's call;
From the school-house and the stee-ple Peals out free-dom to the earth.
Hear the bells of free-dom peal-ing. Man shall har-vest all his grain.
To our God in full thanks-giv-ing, In a song of prayer and praise.
Men of faith who did not fal-ter, Known and un-known, we praise All.

From "Religious Science Hymnal". Used by permission of Dodd, Mead & Co.

Faith of Our Fathers

ST. CATHERINE
Henri F. Hemy
Adapted by James G. Walton

Frederick W. Faber, adapted

1. Faith of our fa - thers, O how great! Hon - or - ing God, and
2. Faith of our fa - thers, We would be Ev - er the sons of
3. Faith of our fa - thers, With us yet! Be in our thoughts lest
home and state; Guard - ing the great - est free - dom known,
lib - er - ty; Grate - ful our thoughts in ev - 'ry prayer
we for - get; Let law and jus - tice ev - er stand,
Born of the vi - sion they had sown;
For the true her - i - tage we share; Faith of our fa - thers,
With God our strong sus - tain - ing hand;
liv - ing still, Be in our mind, our heart, our will. A - men.

Let All Who Enter

(Introit)

Jacqueline Lake

PICARDY, Irr.
Traditional French Melody

Let all who en - ter now keep si - lence, so to feel His
pres - ence here. Raise our thoughts to Him who cre - a - ted
all in per - fect har - mo - ny. God with - in us now for -
ev - er dwell - eth, Our full bless - ings to pro - claim. A-men.

Words used by permission of author.

The Lord Is in His Holy Temple 157

W. H. Bagby, alt. J. H. Fillmore

1. The Lord is in His ho-ly tem-ple; Let earth be-fore Him si-lence keep. In rev-'rence bow, ye loft-y moun-tains, And be Thou still, O won-drous deep!
2. The Lord is in His ho-ly tem-ple; De-clare the Truth in u-ni-ty; Be si-lent in His joy-ful pres-ence, Whose glo-ry fills e-ter-ni-ty.
Refrain
The Lord is in His ho-ly tem-ple; The Lord is in His ho-ly tem-ple. Keep si-lence, Keep si-lence, Keep si-lence be-fore Him. The Lord is in His ho-ly tem-ple.
A-men.

From "Unity Song Selections".

158 Let There Be Peace on Earth

(Let It Begin with Me)

Sy Miller
and Jill Jackson

C Am Dm7 G7 C F Em C
Let there be peace on earth And let it be - gin with
Let peace be - gin with me, Let this be the mo - ment
mp
Dm G7 C B7
me: Let there be peace on earth,
now. With ev - 'ry step I take,
Em B7 G7 1. Am
The peace that was meant to be. With God as our
Let this be my sol - emn vow: To
Em C7 F G7 C Am7
Fa - ther, Broth - ers all are we. Let me
D7 G Am D7 G7
walk with my broth - er In per - fect har - mo - ny.

2. C C+ F
take each mo - ment and live each mo - ment in peace e -

Fdim Am D Fm C E
ter - nal - ly. Let there be

F C C7 F E Am Dm G7 C
peace on earth and let it be - gin with me.

Kum Ba Yah 159

Anon. Anon.

C F C F C
1. Kum ba yah, my Lord, Kum ba yah! Kum ba yah, my Lord, Kum ba
2. Some-one's pray - ing, Lord, Kum ba yah! Some-one's pray - ing, Lord, Kum ba
3. Some-one's sing - ing, Lord, Kum ba yah! Some-one's sing - ing, Lord, Kum ba
G7 C F C F C G7 C
yah! Kum ba yah, my Lord, Kum ba yah! O Lord, Kum ba yah.
yah! Some-one's pray - ing, Lord, Kum ba yah! O Lord, Kum ba yah.
yah! Some-one's sing - ing, Lord, Kum ba yah! O Lord, Kum ba yah.

From "Hymns of Universal Praise." "Kum Ba Yah" means "Come by here".

160

We Go Now in Peace

(A Closing Hymn)

Nadene McClellan

"Leave Me With a Smile"
Arr. by Norman L. Owen

C
1. With the ser - vice end - ing, and our voic - es blend - ing, We go
2. With new thoughts a - bound - ing, and with Love sur - round - ing, We go
E♭dim7 Dm7 G7
now in Peace. (in Peace) With our Christ to guide us,
now in Peace. (in Peace) With our hearts made read - y,
Dm G7 C Cm G7
and our Good sup - plied us, We are blessed with Peace. (with Peace)
and our pur - pose stead - y, We are blessed with Peace. (with Peace)
C C7
When God's will is done, it's right for ev - 'ry - one and all our joys in -
With God's strength sus - tain - ing, and with faith un - wan - ing, cares we now re -

F A7 Dm Cdim C
crease. To our God we raise our voice in grate-ful praise, As
lease. To our God we raise our voice in grate-ful praise, As
D7 1. G7 C 2. G7 C
we go now in Peace.
we go now in Peace.

It is Love

161

Thos. L. McClellan

Thos. L. McClellan

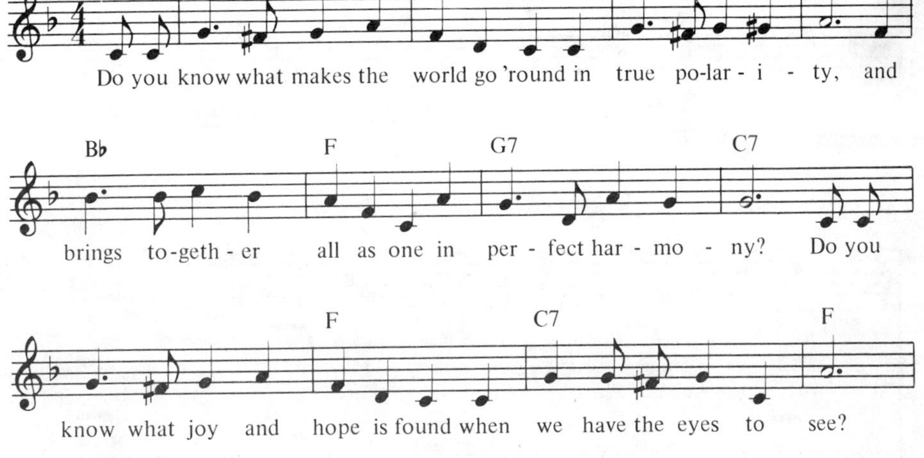
C7 F C7 F
Do you know what makes the world go 'round in true po-lar - i - ty, and
B♭ F G7 C7
brings to-geth - er all as one in per - fect har - mo - ny? Do you
F C7 F
know what joy and hope is found when we have the eyes to see?
B♭ F D7 G7 C7 F
It is Love ex-pressed, it is Love twice blessed, it is Love, it is Love.

162 Doxology

John Murray,
Isaac Watts, & others
OLD HUNDREDTH
Genevan Psalter, 1551
1. Praise God that Good is ev - 'ry - where; Praise
2. From all that dwell be - low the skies Let
3. Praise God in whom all Be - ing is; Praise
God for Love we all may share, For Life that thrills in
songs of hope and faith a - rise; Let peace, good - will on
Him for Word and Form are His; Praise Him, all ye His
you and me; Praise God for Truth that sets us free.
earth be sung Through ev - ery land, by ev - ery tongue.
truth pro - claim; Sing joy - ful praise un - to His name.

Vs. 1 from "Songs for the New Day", United Church of Religious Science.
Vs. 2 from "Hymns for the Celebration of Life", Beacon Press.
Vs. 3 from "Divine Science Hymnal", Divine Science Church.

Declaration Theme Song

Thos. L. McClellan
Thos. L. McClellan
Eb
Bb7
1. Seek and find, with - in Mind, and de - clare
2. Love and Light, Law a - right, are your guide;
Spir - it whole, in the soul, al - ways there.
Re - a - lize, har - mo - nize, faith ap - plied.
For your God and you are one, and you are the liv - ing son;
And the joy that comes to you, let it flow to oth - ers too;
Feel the glow, real - ly know, real - ly care.
Just be - lieve, and re - ceive, and a - bide.

We believe in God, the Living Spirit Almighty: one, indestructible, absolute and self-existent Cause.

We believe this One manifests Itself in and through all creation, but is not absorbed by Its creation.

We believe the manifest universe is the body of God: it is the logical and necessary outcome of the infinite self-knowingness of God.

We believe in the incarnation of the Spirit in man and that all men are incarnations of the One Spirit.

We believe in the eternality, the immortality and the continuity of the individual soul, forever and ever expanding.

We believe that the Kingdom of Heaven is within man and that we experience this Kingdom to the degree that we become conscious of it.

We believe the ultimate goal of life to be a complete emancipation from all discord of every nature, and that this goal is sure to be attained by all.

We believe in the unity of all life, and that the highest God and the innermost God is one God.

We believe that God is personal to all who feel this Indwelling Presence.

We believe in the direct revelation of Truth through the intuitive and spiritual nature of man, and that any man may become a revealer of Truth who lives in close contact with the Indwelling God.

We believe that the Universal Spirit, which is God, operates through a Universal Mind, which is the Law of God: and that we are surrounded by this Creative Mind which receives the direct impress of our thought and acts upon it.

We believe in the healing of the sick through the power of this Mind.

We believe in the control of conditions through the power of this Mind.

We believe in the eternal Goodness, the eternal Loving-Kindness and the eternal Givingness of Life to all.

We believe in our own soul, our own spirit and our own destiny: for we understand that the life of man is God.

– Ernest Holmes

The most precious thing · a man possesses · is his own individuality · as a center of God Consciousness.

> Whatever the mind of man can conceive · and believe · it can achieve.

The word of man · is the law of his life · under the One Great Law · of all life.

> Thou shalt also decree a thing · and it shall be established unto thee · and the light · shall shine on thy ways.

Thoughts are things · they have the power to objectify themselves. Thought lays hold of Causation · and forms real Substance.

> Everyone · automatically attracts to himself · just what he is.

He is richest · who believes that there is a Power to create · and that it contains within Itself · all the details of its creation.

> The more the soul lives · in the light of the Spirit · turned toward that which is above itself · the more creative it becomes.

Spirit works for us · by working through us · it cannot work in any other way.

> For whosoever hath · to him shall be given · and he shall have more abundance · but whosoever hath not · from him shall be taken away · even that he hath.

Seek ye first the kingdom of God · and his righteousness · and all these things · shall be added unto you.

> How precious also · are thy thoughts unto me O God · how great is the sum of them.

Lift up your eyes and look on the fields · for they are white already to harvest. Giving thanks always · for all things · unto God.

Ephesians 5:20
Job 22:28
John 4:35
Matthew 6:33, 13:12
Psalms 139:17
Ernest Holmes
Goethe
Plotinus

All thought is creative · according to the nature · impulse · emotion · or conviction · behind the thought.

> For with the same measure · that ye mete withal · it shall be measured to you again.

Thoughts are not the power · but they do have the invisible Power · flowing through them.

> As man thinketh · in his heart · so is he.

Thought · is reflected as attitude · is expressed as action · is repeated as habit · is established as personality · and becomes the outward measure · of one's livingness.

> To each · life brings the reward of his own visioning · and receptivity.

Life · is not a goblet to be emptied · but a measure to be filled.

> Thou therefore · which teachest another · teachest thou not thyself?
> Chop your own wood · and it will warm you twice.

Whatsoever things are true · honest · just · pure · lovely · of good report · if there be any virtue · and if there be any praise · think on these things.

Luke 6:38
Philippians 4:8
Proverbs 23:7
Romans 2:21
Ernest Holmes
Anonymous

Belief in limitation · is the one and only thing that causes limitations · because we thus impress limitation · upon the creative principle.

> The glowworm · while exploring the dust · never knows that stars are in the sky.

If man takes his images of thought · only from his previous experiences · then he continues in the bondage · which those previous experiences create.

> Whosoever committeth sin · is the servant of sin.

Evil · is not a thing in itself · yet it is more than a belief · it is a solid conviction.

> For from within · out of the heart of men · come evil thoughts · deceit · envy · greed · slander.

By the act of our creative thought · the evil which we experience · is brought into our existence.

> All of our inner conflicts · are a result of a violation · of the natural laws · of self-expression.

God hath made man upright · but they have sought out · many inventions · The only reason man is limited · is that he has not allowed the Divine within him · to more completely express.

> As man realizes his Oneness with Creative Mind · he is released from the bondage of false thinking.

As the inner light dawns · it delivers the outer from bondage.

> The Divine Giver · is also · the Great Forgiver.

Go · and sin no more. Let the evening · forgive the mistakes of the day · and thus win peace for herself.

Ecclesiastes 7:29	Ernest Holmes
John 8:11, 8:34	Rabindranath Tagore
Mark 7:21	Thomas Troward
	Anonymous

Marvel not that I said unto thee · ye must be born again.

Except a man be born again · he cannot see the kingdom of God.

Be not conformed to this world · but be ye transformed · by the renewing of your mind · that ye may prove · what is that good · and acceptable · and perfect will of God.

To be born of the spirit · is to do the will of the Spirit · which is goodness · peace · mercy · justice · and truth. It is conscious union with God.

Be renewed · in the spirit of your mind · put on the new man.

When I was a child · I spake as a child · I understood as a child · I thought as a child · but when I became a man · I put away childish things.

No man putteth a piece of new cloth · unto an old garment · for that which is put in to fill it up · taketh from the garment · and the rent is made worse.

We are continuously living a new life · and when the old and the new · do not fit nicely together · the old · being no longer able to contain the new · should be discarded.

We should serve in newness of spirit · and not in the oldness of the letter.
As we prune away the old · the new growth appears.

For whosoever will save his life · shall lose it · but whosoever will lose his life · for my sake · the same shall save it.

Put off your old nature · and be renewed in the spirit of your mind.

Today is new · and I am newly awakened in it.

A journey of three thousand miles · is begun by a single step.

I Corinthians 13:11
Ephesians 4:22-24
John 3:3, 3:7
Luke 9:24
Matthew 9:16
Romans 7:6, 12:2
Ernest Holmes
Lao-tse

Now the end of the commandment · is charity out of a pure heart · and of a good conscience · and of faith unfeigned.

But let it not be that outward adorning · but let it be · the hidden man of the heart.

Though I speak · with the tongues of men and of angels · and have not charity · I am become as sounding brass · or a tinkling cymbal.

And though I have the gift of prophecy · and understand all mysteries · and all knowledge;

And though I have all faith · so that I could remove mountains · and have not charity · I am nothing.

And though I bestow all my goods · to feed the poor · and though I give my body to be burned · and have not charity · it profiteth me nothing.

Charity suffereth long · and is kind;

Charity envieth not;

Charity vaunteth not itself · is not puffed up;

Doth not behave itself unseemly · seeketh not her own;

Is not easily provoked · thinketh no evil.

Rejoiceth not in iniquity · but rejoiceth in the truth;

Beareth all things · believeth all things,

Hopeth all things · endureth all things.

And now abideth faith · hope ·charity · these three · but the greatest of these · is charity.

I Corinthians 13:1-7, 13:13
I Peter 3:3-4
I Timothy 1:5

As a son of God · man has the ability to choose his thoughts · and is unified with a Divine Principle · which produces his choice.

> Not by might · nor by power · but by my spirit · saith the Lord.

It is the spirit that quickeneth · the flesh profiteth nothing · the words that I speak unto you · they are spirit · and they are life.

> The Mind must conceive · before the Creative Energy can produce · we must supply the avenue · through which It can work.

We must have a mental equivalent · of the thing we desire.

> To know what you know · and know what you don't know · is characteristic of one who knows.

It is the lack of purpose · that deprives us of power.

> A double-minded man is unstable · in all his ways.

And if a house be divided against itself · that house cannot stand.

> Through wisdom is a house builded · and by understanding it is established.

Each man is the center · of his own universe · and has the power · by directing his own thought · to control all things therein.

> Ask · and it shall be given you · seek · and ye shall find · knock · and it shall be opened unto you.

So shall my word be · that goeth forth out of my mouth · it shall not return to me void · but it shall accomplish that which I please · and it shall prosper in the thing whereto I send it.

Isaiah 55:11
James 1:8
John 6:63
Mark 3:25
Matthew 7:7
Proverbs 24:3
Zechariah 4:6
Confucius
Ernest Holmes
Thomas Troward

Christ is the image of God · the Man that Spirit conceives · God never begot but one Son · but the Eternal is forever begetting · the only begotten.

Christ is a principle · the embodiment of Divine Sonship · which has come to all people · with varying degrees of power · in all ages.

In the personality of Jesus · there was a greater individual awareness · and incarnation · of the Universal Presence.

And the child grew · and waxed strong in spirit · filled with wisdom · and the grace of God was upon him.

And Jesus said · "Why callest thou me good? · There is none good but one · that is God."

"He that believeth on me · believeth not on me · but on him that sent me. And he that seeth me · seeth him that sent me."

"Believest thou not that I am in the Father · and the Father in me? The words that I speak unto you · I speak not of myself · but the Father that dwelleth in me · he doeth the works."

Asking the disciples · Jesus said · "Who do men say that the Son of man is?" And they said · "Some say that thou art John the Baptist · or one of the prophets."

He saith unto them · "But who do you say that I am?" And Simon Peter said · "Thou art the Christ · the Son of the living God."

Jesus answered · "Blessed art thou · Simon Bar-jona · for flesh and blood · hath not revealed it unto thee · but my Father · which is in heaven."

"And I say · also unto thee · that thou art."

John 12:44-45, 14:10 Meister Eckhart
Luke 2:40 Ernest Holmes
Matthew 16:13-18, 19:17

Communion with the Spirit · is one of the greatest privileges of life. It is entering into the presence of Spirit · silently · quietly · and alone · and listening and feeling · until that Presence is real to us.

> Inner prayer or communion · is essential · to the conscious well-being · of the soul.

This inner communion · is a constant recognition of our relationship · to that Presence in which we live · and move · and have our being.

> We cannot have faith without communion · because it is this communion · that gives us the faith.

The power of prayer is generated · when we consciously direct our thinking · toward a specific and edifying purpose. The essence of prayer · is faith and acceptance.

> Faith and acceptance · is the true motive power · that attracts and magnifies · the hidden potentialities of Life.

Prayer is not an act · of overcoming Gods reluctance · but should be an active acceptance · of his highest willingness.

> In effective prayer · I realize that a Power greater than I am · consciously acts with creative Intelligence · upon my word.

Prayer should be understood · not as a mere mechanical recitation of formula · but as a mystical elevation · an absorption of consciousness · in the contemplation of a principle · both permeating and transcending our world.

> If one will set in quiet contemplation of good · as an inner experience · he will experience the good · which he contemplates.

In quietude and meditation · there is an inward absorption of Universal Life · that brings relaxation · releasement · and renewal.

> In communion and thanksgiving · there is a realization and knowingness · that brings assurance · confidence · and peace.

In stillness now · I seek and find · the Wisdom of the greater Mind.

Alexis Carrel
Ernest Holmes
Anonymous

Now faith · is the assurance of things hoped for · the conviction of things not seen.

Faith is a mental attitude · so inwardly embodied · that the mind can no longer deny it.

Pure faith is a spiritual conviction · it is the acquiescence of the mind · the embodiment of an idea · the acceptance of a concept.

Faith is built upon belief · acceptance · and trust.

For if there be first a willing mind · it is accepted · according to that a man hath · and not according to that he hath not.

There is a vast difference · between holding thoughts · and knowing the truth.

Keep thy heart with all diligence · for out of it · are the issues of life.

Cast not away therefore your confidence · which hath great recompense of reward.

No man · having put his hand to the plough · and looking back · is fit for the kingdom of God.

In faith we turn within · and find God.

We must trust the invisible · for it is the sole cause · of that which is visible.

The faith waiting in the heart of a seed · promises a miracle of life · it cannot prove.

According to your faith · be it done unto you.

II Corinthians 8:12
Hebrew 10:35, 11:1
Luke 9:62
Matthew 9:29
Proverbs 4:23
Ernest Holmes
Rabindranath Tagore

I put thee in remembrance · that thou stir up the gift of God · which is in thee.

That he would grant you · according to the riches of his glory · to be strengthened with might · by his Spirit in the inner man.

Now we have received · not the spirit of the world · but the spirit which is of God · that we might know the things · that are freely given to us · of God.

God is a principle · personified in each of us. Spirituality is the atmosphere · of this Principle.

The Life of God · is the eternal and perfect Essence · of all things. That life is God's gift to me. Therefore · Its fullness is within me · ready to manifest through me · as I consciously partake of It.

The knowledge that the great I AM · is ever available · gives me an increasing capacity to draw upon It · and to become inwardly aware · of the presence of Spirit.

As man sees the glory of God in Life · so shall Life reflect back to him that same glory. The image and its reflection become one · even as the Father and Son are one · in glory · honor · majesty · and might.

If I honor myself · my honor is nothing. It is my Father that honoreth me.

The branch cannot bear fruit · by itself.

The Father that dwelleth in me · he doeth the works.

Now unto him · that is able to do exceeding abundantly · above all that we ask or think · according to the power that worketh in us · unto him be glory.

I Coronthians 2:12
Ephesians 3:16, 3:20-21
John 8:54, 14:10, 15:4
II Timothy 1:6
Ernest Holmes

I am Alpha and Omega · the beginning and the ending · saith the Lord · which is · and which was · and which is to come · the Almighty.

All the Power there is · all the Presence there is · all the Love there is · and the only God there is · is omnipresent.

There is a universal Life and Energy · that finds an outlet · in and through all that is energized · and through everything that lives.

We are surrounded · by an intelligent force and substance · from which all things come.

There is a Presence in the universe which knows · a Law which acts · and a Creation which corresponds. This is the Divine Principle.

God does not acquire qualities · God is the Essence · the quality is merely the way · It manifests Itself.

The nature of God · is creative and constructive · but God is not absorbed · in His creation.

I am the Lord · I change not.

Whatever is · is in God · and nothing can exist or be conceived · without God. God himself is One · Single · One only · He is the Creator · the Source of every soul.

God is the Life-Principle · He is the Speech and the Mind · He is the Truth · He is Immortal.

Lo · I am with you always · even unto the end of the world · Be still and know · that I am God.

Malachi 3:6	Hinduism
Matthew 28:20	Ernest Holmes
Psalms 46:10	Baruch Spinoza
Revelations 1:8	Upanishad

In the beginning was the Word · and the Word was with God · and the Word was God.

> And God said · let there be light · and there was light.

And God saw everything that he had made · and behold · it was very good.

> All things were made by him · and without him was not anything made · that was made.

God as an infinite Creator · is eternally imparting his Nature · to his creation.

> God is the same · yesterday · today · and tomorrow · but within this changeless One · all changing forms exist.

All creation · is from Idea to Form. Forms come and go · but the Power back of them remains forever · and is changeless.

> In our physical system · there is a sum total of energies that remains constant · through all changes that might occur.

The perfect and unchangeable life · of the Divine Spirit · overflows in an incessant stream · of creative activity. He hath made everything beautiful · in his time.

> O Lord · how manifold are they works! In wisdom hast thou made them all. The earth is full of thy riches.

This is the day · which the Lord hath made · we will rejoice and be glad in it.

Ecclesiastes 3:11	Albert Einstein
Genesis 1:3, 1:31	Ernest Holmes
John 1:1, 1:3	Plotinus
Psalms 104:24, 118:24	Thomas Troward

So God created man in his own image · in the image of God created he him.

> For as the Father · hath life in himself · so hath he given to the Son · to have life in himself.

Man is made out of · and from · Life. As effect must partake of the nature of its cause · so man must partake of the Divine Nature · from which he springs.

> There is incarnated in each of us · that Divine Spark · which contains the whole of the nature · of God.

The Spirit of God hath made me · and the breath of the Almighty hath given me life.

> We use a Power greater than we are. It is our strength · but we ourselves are not that power. There is one Life · behind all that lives.

Out of all the variations of life · the infinite variety of color · and form · and people · one Power is working · one Life is expressing · one Mind is animating · one Presence flowing through · and one Law controlling.

> The basis of all scientific work · is the conviction · that the world is an ordered · and comprehensive unity.

And there are diversities of operations · but it is the same God · which worketh all in all · There are diversities of gifts · but the same Spirit.

> There is one body · and one spirit · one God and Father of all · who is above all · and through all · and in you all.

God worketh in each · through a conscious attitude · of gratitude and receptivity. Joy · is the most infallible sign · of the Presence of God.

I Corinthians 12:4, 12:6
Ephesians 4:4-6
Genesis 1:27
Job 33:4
John 5:26
Albert Einstein
Pierre Teilhard de Chardin
Ernest Holmes
Anonymous

Evolution of man · involves the unfoldment of personality · the enlightenment of the soul · the illumination of the spirit.

The evolution of the individual · can come only to the degree that the individual himself · purposes to let Life operate through him.

There is a law of unfoldment in man · which says he can advance · only by going from where he is · to the place where he would like to be.

God does not work in all hearts alike · but according to the preparation · and sensitivity · in each one.

We should work · not with anxiety · but with expectancy · not by coercion · but by conviction · not through compulsion · but in a state of conscious recognition · and receptivity.

There is a pace · a rhythm · and a harmony of Life · to which we should attune our thoughts · and actions.

To everything there is a season · and a time to every purpose · under the heaven.

There is nothing so powerful in the world · as an idea · whose time has come.

The spiral of life is upward. Evolution carries us forward · not backward. The stimulus and growth · comes from being challenged.

Man has been given the power of creative thought · by which he has a freedom of choice · in shaping his own experiences.

Positive and negative thinking · are merely two ways of using the same mind · through the power of choice.

At all times we radiate and attract. To speak the word with authority · there must be no doubt in consciousness.

Choose you this day · whom ye will serve.

Ecclesiastes 3:1	Ernest Holmes
Joshua 24:15	Victor Hugo
Meister Eckhart	Anonymous

There is ever a song of life · of beauty · of peace · and we should learn to sing it.

A merry heart doeth good · like medicine · but a broken spirit drieth the bones.

We have a right to any happiness · of which we can conceive · provided that happiness hurts no one · and is in keeping · with the nature of progressive life.

Take therefore no thought for the morrow · for the morrow shall take thought · for the things of itself.

Though we travel the world over · to find the beautiful · we must carry it with us · or we find it not.

As far as mind extends · so far extends heaven.

Happy is the man that findeth wisdom · and the man that getteth understanding.

The blessing of the Lord · it maketh rich · and he addeth no sorrow with it.

Always there is the Eternal Voice · forever whispering within our ear · that thing which causes the eternal quest · that thing which forever sings and sings.

A new heart also will I give you · and a new spirit will I put within you.

Arise · shine · for thy light is come · and the glory of the Lord · is risen upon thee.

I will sing a new song unto thee · O God.

Rejoice in the Lord always · and again I say · Rejoice!

Ezekiel 36:26
Isaiah 60:1
Matthew 6:34
Philippians 4:4
Proverbs 3:13, 10:22, 17:22
Psalms 144:9
Ralph Waldo Emerson
Ernest Holmes
Upanishad

Healing · is the substitution of Truth · for sense testimony. The creativity of Universal Mind · and one's attunement to it · brings the healing idea · and the expressed action.

> Surely that which has the intelligence to create · has also the will and ability · to sustain.

No matter how imperfect the appearance may be · or painful · or discordant · there is still an underlying Perfection · an inner Wholeness · a complete and Perfect Life · which is God.

> The basis of all healing · is a change in belief. Our belief does not change Reality · it merely changes our position in Reality.

Treatment is not willing things to happen · it is to provide within ourselves · an avenue through which they may happen.

> Bodies and conditions never move · they are always moved upon.

Let the feeling of well-being circulate deep within you · removing all tension and congestion. Focus on the healing Life forces · responding to your call.

> For God hath not given us the spirit of fear · but of power · and of love · and a sound mind.

Is any among you afflicted? Let him pray.

> Pray to thy Father in secret · and thy Father which seeth in secret · shall reward thee openly.

What things soever ye desire · when ye pray · believe that ye receive them · and ye shall have them.

> Each one is to ask · for that which is in unity with Life · but let him ask in faith · nothing wavering.

Physician heal thyself. This day declare thy good. Go in peace and be whole.

James 1:6, 5:13	Ernest Holmes
Luke 4:23	Raymond K. Lilley
Mark 5:34, 11:24	Thomas Troward
Matthew 6:6	Anonymous
II Timothy 1:7	

This is the promise that he hath promised us · even eternal life.

Yea though I walk through the valley · of the shadow of death · I will fear no evil · for Thou art with me.

Whither shall I go from thy spirit? Or whither shall I flee from thy presence?

If I ascend up into heaven · Thou art there · if I make my bed in hell · behold Thou art there.

If I take the wings of the morning · and dwell in the uttermost parts of the sea · even there shall thy hand lead me · and thy right hand shall hold me.

We are born of eternal day · and the Spiritual Sun shall never set · upon the glory of the soul · for it is the coming forth of God · into Self-expression.

Man · the real man · is birthless · deathless · changeless · and God as man · in man · is man. Creator and creation · constitute one indivisible Wholeness.

The highest God · and the innermost God · is one and the same God.

We are not going to attain immortality · we are now immortal. Death is but a passing to a higher sphere · of life and action.

And so we prepare · not to die · but to live · not for survival · but for fulfillment of being.

Our contention · is not that dead men live again · but that living man never dies. A consciousness of continuity is finite · but continuity itself is infinite.

Resurrection is the Power of Life · always present · ever creative · ever new. Life and Its resurrection is now. I turn to Life in reverence · hope · and joy.

And this is the record · that God hath given to us eternal life · and this life is in his Son.

I John 2:25, 5:11 — Ernest Holmes
Psalms 23:4, 139:7-10 — Oswald Jefferson

Thine · O Lord · is the greatness · and the power · and the glory · and the victory · and the majesty · for all that is in the heaven · and in the earth · is thine.

Thy kingdom · is an everlasting kingdom · and thy dominion endureth · throughout all generations.

When anyone heareth the word of the kingdom · and understandeth it not · then cometh the wicked one · and catcheth away that which was sown in the heart.

But he that received seed into the good ground · is he that heareth the word · and understandeth it · which also beareth fruit.

Wisdom is the principal thing · therefore get wisdom · and with all thy getting · get understanding.

For if I pray in an unknown tongue · my spirit prayeth · but my understanding is unfruitful.

Understanding · is a well-spring of life · unto him that hath it. He that will · let him take the water of life freely.

The gift of heaven is Life · and not death · Love · and not hate · Peace · and not confusion.

The Law · reflects our attitudes · but the Spirit · urges us into righteousness. And the work of righteousness shall be peace · and the effect of righteousness · quietness · and assurance. For righteousness is using the Law aright.

The kingdom of God · cometh not with observation · neither shall they say lo here! or lo there! For behold · the kingdom of God · is within you.

For the kingdom of God · is not meat and drink · but righteousness · and peace · and joy in the Holy Spirit.

I Corinthians 14:14
I Chronicles 29:11
Isaiah 32:17
Luke 12:32, 17:20-21
Matthew 13:19, 13:23
Revelation 22:17
Proverbs 4:7, 16:22
Psalms 145:3
Romans 14:17
Ernest Holmes

I have said Ye are gods · and all of you · are children of the Most High. The Spirit itself beareth witness · with our spirit · that we are the children of God.

We are not separated from Life · neither is It separated from us · but we are separate entities in it · individualized centers of God-Consciousness.

The Divine Incarnation · is inherent in our nature. We are immersed in an Infinite Knowingness.

The Spirit of Truth · or true Reality · is changeless and eternal · and its activity extends to everything · and is present everywhere.

Spirit is Conscious Mind · and is the Power which knows Itself · and in us · constitutes our Self-Awareness · It is Conscious Being.

Spirit is First Cause · or God · The Absolute Essence of all that is · and is the Principle of Unity · back of all things. It is the Great or Universal I AM.

The Christ · represents the highest nature in man · or the Universal I AM · in every man. The God of all · is personal to each.

The spiritual genius of Jesus · perceived that the Universal I AM · is reproduced in the individual I.

Though ye believe not me · believe the works · that ye may know · and believe · that the Father is in me and I in him.

And I will pray the Father · and he shall give you another comforter · that he may abide with you forever · Even the Spirit of Truth.

At that day · ye shall know that I am in my Father · and ye are in me · and I in you.

John 10:38, 14:16-17, 14:20 Ernest Holmes
Psalms 82:6 Plotinus
Romans 8:16

Thou shalt love the Lord thy God · with all thy heart · and with all thy soul · and with all thy strength · and with all thy mind · and thy neighbor as thyself.

> Eye hath not seen · nor ear heard · neither have entered into the heart of man · the things which God hath prepared · for them that love him.

Love is the prime moving power · of the Creating Spirit. It is the self-givingness of the Spirit · through the desire of Life to express Itself · in terms of creation.

> Reverence for Life · comprises the whole ethic of love · in its deepest and highest sense. Take time to see · appreciate · and enjoy the beauty · and love · around you each day.

He needs no other rosary · whose life is strung with beads of loving thought. Love is the grandest healing power on earth · for love is the outpouring of the Spirit.

> Love is patient and kind · is not jealous or boastful · is not arrogant or rude.

Love does not insist on its own way · is not irritable or resentful · it does not rejoice at wrong · but rejoices in the right.

> Joy to forgive · and joy to be forgiven · hang level in the balance of love.

Why beholdest thou the mote · that is in thy brother's eye · but considerest not the beam · that is in thine own eye?

> Search thine own heart. What paineth thee in others · in thyself may be · for the light one throws on others · is generated in one's own soul.

Put on love · which binds everything together in perfect harmony. For this is the message · that ye heard from the beginning · that we should love one another.

Colossians 3:14	Richard Garnett
I Corinthians 2:9	Ernest Holmes
I John 3:11	Albert Schweitzer
Luke 10:27	Thomas Troward
Matthew 7:3	John Greenleaf Whittier
Anonymous	Zoroastrian Scriptures

Negation may be an experience · and a fact · it can never be an ultimate truth. Truth cannot express in terms · contrary to its own nature.

> For we can do nothing against the truth · but for the truth.

If you continue in my word · then are ye my disciples indeed · and you shall know the truth · and the truth shall make you free.

> Every Thought of Doubt is · in effect · the utterance of a word which produces negative results · by the same law · by which the Word of Faith produces positive ones.

Law is Mind in action · and is a blind force. The same force · that makes man sick · poor · or miserable · can heal · enrich · or make happy.

> Mind is potential energy · thought is the dynamic force · which produces the activity.

As we fill our mind · with the Truth of Being · the harmful forces of fear · hate · inferiority · and guilt · are transformed · to an exalted new potential.

> By a change in direction · and force of action · we open the door to releasement and renewal. The potential of destructive power · becomes curative · protective · and regenerative.

Fear is a mental attitude · a belief in limitation · and is a denial that the Divine · is the Center and Source of all good.

> Fear not · for it is your Father's good pleasure · to give you the kingdom.

It is only when the intellect is no longer obstructed · by negative emotional reactions · arising out of the experiences of doubt and fear · that the word of the mouth can immediately bear fruit.

> We turn from the confusion of fear · to the certainty of faith · and our good is made manifest.

Be not overcome of evil · but overcome evil with good.

II Corinthians 13:8	Ernest Holmes
John 8:31-32	Alvin D. St. John
Luke 12:32	Thomas Troward
Romans 12:31	Anonymous

There is no obstruction · or fact · that can stop or exhaust · the limitless flow of life.

Because certain facts in our experience · let us know when we are not in tune with life · they should be recognized and not denied.

Facts do not rule · but declare our level of understanding · receptivity · and response.

Nothing is real to us · unless we make it real.

What we demonstrate today · tomorrow · and the next day · is not as important as the tendency · which our thought is taking.

The great thing in this world · is not so much where we stand · as in what direction we are moving.

Learn the landmarks of the forest first · and the trail through the trees · will be swift and sure.

Life fills all space · and Spirit animates every form · but only that which each one accepts · is his to use.

He that is faithful · in that which is least · is faithful also in much.

We should realize · that potential remains potential · until it expresses itself.

The fullness of Life's potential · is accomplished through the uncovering · of that which is already within us.

With spiritual convictions · come all else.

What we do not act up to · we do not really believe.

Luke 16:10
Ernest Holmes
Oliver Wendell Holmes
Raymond K. Lilley
Thomas Troward
Anonymous

Spiritual understanding · is a process of self-awakening.

That within us · which enables us to be aware · is the Spirit · that is incarnated in us.

The essence of Life is ever present · we neither make it · nor destroy it.

That which is born of the Spirit · is spirit.

No man ever walks life's road alone · there is ever his inner self.

Whoever knows the all · but fails to know himself · lacks everything.

Which of you by taking thought · can add one cubit unto his stature?

You experience the power · and the goodness of pure Spirit · in such degree as you accept · believe in · and feel it.

We are not depending on a reed · shaken by the wind · but on the principle of life Itself.

Intuition is God in man · revealing to him · the Realities of Being.

Intuition knows · It deals with essence rather than appearances · and is not discolored by human argument · or deductions.

For now · we see through a glass darkly · but then · face to face.

Now · I know in part · but then · shall I know even as also I am known.

I Corinthians 13:12
John 3:6
Matthew 6:27
Gospel according to Thomas p. 4
Ernest Holmes

There is a spirit in man · and the inspiration of the Almighty · giveth him understanding.

Understanding · is the key to true salvation · for it reveals Truth · through a new measure · of awareness and response.

Behold · now is the accepted time · behold · now is the day of salvation.

God hath from the beginning · chosen you to salvation · through sanctification by the Spirit · and belief in the truth.

Teach me O God · not to torture myself · condemning myself through stifling reflections · but rather · teach me to breathe deeply in faith.

When I shall · with my whole self cleave to Thee · I shall nowhere have sorrow.

For we are saved by hope · but hope that is seen is not hope · for what a man seeth · why doth he yet hope for?

But if we hope for that we see not · then do we with patience · wait for it.

Right thought · constantly poured into consciousness · will eventually purify it. These things have I spoken unto you · that my joy might remain in you · and that your joy might be full.

Each has within himself · this guide to truth · to reason · to beauty · to right action · to certainty · and to peace.

He hath showed thee O man · what is good · and what doth the Lord require of thee · but to do justly · and to love mercy · and to walk humbly with thy God.

II Corinthians 6:2
Job 32:8
John 15:11
Micah 6:8
Romans 8:24-25
II Thessalonians 2:13
Ernest Holmes
Soren Aabye Kierkegaard
St. Augustine
Anonymous

Come unto me · all ye that labor and are heavy laden · and I will give you rest.

Draw nigh to God · and he will draw nigh to you.

For thou Lord art good · and ready to forgive · and plenteous in steadfast love · unto all them that call upon thee.

God is our refuge and strength · a very present help in trouble.

And ye shall seek me · and find me · when ye shall search for me · with all your heart.

If therefore thine eye be single · thy whole body · shall be full of light.

Perfect trust in God within · is the secret of relaxation · rest · and renewal.

In quiet · and in confidence · shall be your strength.

Thou wilt keep him in perfect peace · whose mind is stayed on thee · because he trusteth in thee.

Isaiah 26:3, 30:15
James 4:8
Jeremiah 29:13
Matthew 6:22, 11:28
Psalms 46:1, 86:5
Ernest Holmes

For this cause came I into the world · that I should bear witness · unto the truth.

Invariance under transformation · is the deepest test · of significant reality.

Truth · is self-existent reality · unchanging and everlasting.

Wherever truth is proclaimed · God is speaking.

Knowledge · is nothing but the continual burning up of error · to set free the light of Truth.

Truth is that which is · and can have nothing · outside of itself.

Unless the invisible thought · and desire of man · is in line with truth · his acts will fall into error.

And some fell among the thorns · and the thorns sprang up with it · and choked it.

And some fell on good ground · and sprang up and bare fruit · a hundredfold.

You ask · and receive not · because ye ask amiss.

Merely to abstain from wrong thinking · is not enough · there must be active right thinking.

I am not bound to succeed · but I am bound to live up to · what light I have.

Knowing the truth · is a process of gradual unfoldment · of the inner self. When the student is ready · the teacher will appear.

Truth · is the summit of being. Justice · is the application of it to affairs.

Let us therefore follow after the things · which make for peace · and things wherewith · one may edify another.

James 4:3
John 18:37
Luke 8:7-8
Romans 14:19
Donald Hatch Andrews
Ralph Waldo Emerson
Ernest Holmes
Abraham Lincoln
Oriental Philosophy
Rabindranath Tagore

There is one Energy · back of all that is energized.

In the spiritual world · there is distinction without division · The part in a sense · contains the whole · Each soul is universal.

All emerge from the One · whose Being is ever present · and whose Life · robed in numberless forms · is manifest throughout all creation.

There will ever remain · the one absolute certainty · that we are ever in the Presence · of the Infinite Energy · from which all things proceed.

The world of multiplicity · does not contradict the world of Unity · for the many live in the One.

Man is a spirit · while God is The Spirit.

We lie in the lap of immense intelligence · which makes us organs of its activity · and receivers of its truth.

Know ye not · that ye are the temples of God · and that the Spirit of God · dwelleth in you?

We dwell in him · and he in us · because he hath given us · of his Spirit.

I Corinthians 3:16	Ernest Holmes
I John 4:13	Plotinus
Ralph Waldo Emerson	Herbert Spencer

Man's mind · should swing from inspiration to action · from contemplation to accomplishment · from prayer to performance.

> For as the body without spirit · is dead · so faith without works · is dead also.

Behold also the ships · which though they be so great · and are driven of fierce winds · yet are they turned about with a very small rudder · wherever the will of the pilot directs.

> Now therefore perform the doing of it · that as there was a readiness to will · so there may be a performance also · out of that which ye have.

Therefore · to him that knoweth to do good · and doeth it not · to him it is sin. For if a man thinks himself to be something · when he is nothing · he deceiveth himself.

> Be not deceived · God is not mocked · for whatsoever a man soweth · that shall he also reap.

You cannot help men permanently · by doing for them what they could · and should do · for themselves.

> But let every man prove his own work · then shall he have rejoicing · in himself alone · and not in another.

Who learns and learns · and acts not what he knows · is one who plows and plows · and never sows.

> But who looketh into the perfect law of liberty · and continueth therein · he being not a forgetful hearer · but a doer of the work · this man shall be blessed in his deed.

And God is able · to make all grace abound toward you · that ye · always having all sufficiency in all things · may abound to every good work.

II Corinthians 8:11, 9:8	Ernest Holmes
James 1:25, 2:26, 3:4, 4:17	Hugh Magill
Galations 6:3-4, 6:7	Anonymous